LEGORRETA + LEGORRETA

Rizzoli
NEW YORK

First published in the United States of America in 2004
by Rizzoli International Publications, Inc.
300 Park Avenue South
New York, NY 10010
www.rizzoliusa.com

Copyright © 2003 by Area Editores, S.A. de C.V.
Montes Urales 632 P.B.
Mexico City, Mexico, 11000
Tel. (52 55) 5095-2390
www.areaeditores.com

ISBN: 0-8478-2598-1

Library of Congress Catalog Control Number: 2003111680

Editorial coordination

Laura Laviada-Checa

Editing and proofreading

Carlos Méndez

Photography

Lourdes Legorreta (Architecture)

Graciela Iturbide (Portraits)

Design

Estudio la fe ciega

Jacket:

House in Hawaii, Maui, Hawaii, 2002.

Photographed by Katsuhisa Kida.

2003 2004 2005 2006 2007/ 10 9 8 7 6 5 4 3 2 1

Printed in Japan

"My thoughts last night, after seeing the magnificence, the generosity of space, and the exquisite taste proclaimed by your new office, has left me the impression that the architect in you has entered a second stage of his creative life: that of consolidation of a great talent. I think I know something of your moral virtues and I hope this opinion will encourage you not to interrupt your journey. The road ahead is not long but endless."

— José Villagrán

"When walking through the spaces Ricardo Legorreta has created, one is never alone; in the air, in the sounds, in the color of one wall and the size of another, in the wooden floors, in the railing of a window, in the deliberate shadow falling on a terrace, in the long blue corridor or a wall sheltering a door, on each corner, even in the light and scents, there is a signal, an unreachable place, a challenge, a voice."

— Ángeles Mastreta

"You should learn to laugh at yourself." This is an old and truthful saying. We architects shouldn't take ourselves so seriously. It is important for us to understand that we are simple human beings. We want to design for the good of people, contribute to their happiness, complement the work of God, and, most of all, assume that we are not important. We have to attempt great things and still be able to laugh at ourselves. To the extent we do that, we feel we are creating an architecture that is more human and free."

— Legorreta + Legorreta

Contents

16   **Ricardo Legorreta:** Architecture: The Passion to Give, to Create, and to Love
24   **Víctor Legorreta:** I Have Lived Surrounded by Architecture
68   **Richard Rogers:** Legorreta's Architecture
114   **Fumihiko Maki:** Legorreta's Universe

28   WORKS AND PROJECTS 1997–2003

28   Ricardo Legorreta House
40   Visual Arts Center, Santa Fe
58   House in Israel
70   House in Fort Lauderdale
78   Dormitories, University of Chicago
88   Dormitories, Stanford University
94   Los Patios I and II Residential Compound
100   Telmex Technology Center
102   Televisa Santa Fe
112   Lomas House
116   House in Brazil
124   House in Japan
136   Mexican Pavilion for Expo 2000
144   Room for Milan Furniture Fair
146   Sheraton Abandoibarra Hotel
148   House of the 15 Patios
164   Reno House
176   Technological Museum of Innovation
182   House in El Tamarindo
194   EGADE – Business Administration Graduate School
206   American University in Cairo
208   Apartment in Mexico City
214   House in Hawaii
226   Chiron Life & Science Laboratories
234   El Roble Office Building
242   Public Housing Projects
244   Cabernet House
252   Hacienda in São Paulo
254   House Near a Lake
262   Juárez Square
264   Víctor Legorreta House
272   Zandra Rhodes Museum
276   ITESM Santa Fe

290   CHRONOLOGY OF WORKS 1963–2003

296   Ricardo and Víctor Legorreta: Lives and Works
298   Associates and Friends

ARCHITECTURE CANNOT BE DEFINED WITH WORDS

IT IS BEST EXPERIENCED THROUGH EMOTIONS

THROUGHOUT OUR LIVES, WE HAVE COME TO REALIZE THAT IN SPITE OF

OUR SUCCESSES AND FAILURES, OUR TRUE VALUES REMAIN UNCHANGED

Architecture: The Passion to Give, to Create, and to Love

There was no artistic tradition in my family, but my parents bred in me an immense love of Mexico and a profound respect for humanistic values. As part of my typical Mexican upbringing, my education was anything but unconventional. My naturally rebellious character led me to challenge my surroundings and the social status quo of my country and the world around me. As a true romantic, I dreamed of contributing something to the world.

I don't recall when I decided to become an architect. Maybe it was sometime during my frequent trips as a boy to pueblos and haciendas in Mexico that I began to develop an aesthetic sense; here, too, I experienced freedom and the Mexican humanism that was embodied so well by my father. Within that environment, I learned that giving and serving others was to become my life's work.

My childhood education and family upbringing adhered to a very strict and conventional criteria, which not only clashed with my rebellious nature, but which were contrary to what I admired most about the Mexican people. My life changed abruptly when I enrolled in the Universidad Nacional Autónoma de México (UNAM). From that moment, my life transformed itself from one that was contained within a controlled environment to one that would develop in an open, challenging, almost libertine university campus. I attended the campus at the Centro Histórico (Historic Center) in Mexico City, and it was there where I truly understood the profound implication and meaning of being Mexican.

I was fortunate to learn from and work with the great masters of Mexican architecture during the 1950s. Given my strict and structured upbringing, I was especially attracted to the personality and character of José Villagrán, the leader of the Mexican modernist movement.

A victim of my own pride, I didn't want to take advantage of the friendship between my father and José Villagrán, and so I began to work, while still at school and during my free time, as a draftsman for Villagrán. There, I learned the true meaning of my profession's ethical values, which call for architecture to provide a service to users and not to be mistaken for a monument to its creator. The architect is responsible for consciously allocating the resources that are given to him by the state, by society, or by an individual. Villagrán was an educated man, a true scholar who opened my eyes to the universal nature of knowledge. He enabled me to understand the important role that Mexican culture plays within the context of universal culture.

This epiphany in conjunction with my father's teachings and his role as my friend and guide became the building blocks for my future. However, there was still a fundamental void in my professional life that needed to be filled. My ability to dream, as well as my romantic and creative yearning, was being compromised by austerity and asceticism.

After twelve years of collaboration, at the end of which Villagrán and I became partners, I was forced to leave my teacher and mentor. As soon as I was working independently, I was put through one of my life's greatest challenges: being in top shape, I fell ill to a life-threatening infection that nearly took my life in just a few hours. After battling death for a month, I miraculously began to heal, and, at the end of a long recovery, I became a different man. I understood that life's purpose is to serve, to love, and to give, and that time is the most important gift we have.

Although I was physically weakened after this experience, my energy was overpowering and I decided to throw myself with all of the passion and strength that I was capable of mustering, to accomplish my ideals. I discovered a new life, and I realized that architecture without passion is worthless.

During the beginning of my new life, I invited my friend and colleague Noé Castro to embark on an adventure with me. Throughout the years, Noé has become my partner, my adviser, my supporter, and my best friend. I would not have accomplished anything without Noé.

My first clients were very supportive and waited patiently for my physical recovery. Soon, I was able to create and build what I consider to be my first authentic project. In the Automex Factory, I was able to incorporate the essence of Mexican haciendas. In conjunction with Mathias Goeritz, I began to collaborate with painters and sculptors. I discovered the great value of architecture designed for its end users, as evidenced by the workers in Automex Factory, who were much happier in their new environment. Almost immediately, I was assigned one of my life's most important projects: to design a modern commercial complex in an area covering 30,000 square meters bordering Chapultepec Park, the most important park in Mexico City.

At that moment I celebrated life and my artistic freedom and I literally exclaimed, "Viva Mexico!" Looking back, I still don't know how I managed to convince the owners to build what I named La casa de México. My proposal was to build a hotel that would revolutionize the spaces, the colors, the light, and the romanticism characteristic of Mexico. With full support, I dedicated four years of my life to realizing this project. But the beginning was tough, and I learned that not everyone is a prophet in their own land. However, in spite of harsh national criticism, the international respect received by the project was responsible for its ultimate success. At that moment, I had realized one of my greatest dreams: to promote Mexican architecture to achieve international recognition.

What began as an adventure for Noé and myself started to take form. All of my energy and devotion was concentrated on my work, and soon my endless passion took a toll on my personal life. New work started to flow our way, which enabled me to grasp the potential of Mexican architecture and to be able to demonstrate the universal nature of Mexican culture. Throughout ten years of intense work, and with Noé's full support, we put together a team based on friendship, which was able to carry out a wide variety of projects such as houses, factories, hotels, and commercial and urban complexes. The successful completion of these projects made me realize, that regardless of my capabilities, my ideals were important and worth living and fighting for. This is when I understood that in life, perseverance and enthusiasm are more important than accomplishments.

FROM LEFT TO RIGHT, TOP TO BOTTOM:

SMITH KLINE & FRENCH LABORATORIES, MEXICO CITY., MEXICO, 1964; AUTOMEX FACTORY, TOLUCA, MEXICO, 1964; OFFICE BUILDING, MONTERREY, MEXICO, 1995; RENAUL FACILITIES, DURANGO, MEXICO, 1985; MONTALBÁN HOUSE, CALIFORNIA, UNITED STATES, 1985; WESTIN REGINA HOTEL (FORMERLY CONRAD), CANCÚN, MEXICO, 1991; LEGORRETA ARQUITECTOS, MEXICO CITY, MEXICO, 1966; METROPOLITAN CATHEDRAL OF MANAGUA, NICARAGUA, 1994; MARCO MUSEUM OF CONTEMPORARY ART, MONTERREY, MEXICO, 1991; WESTIN BRISAS HOTEL (FORMERLY CAMINO REAL), IXTAPA, MEXICO, 1981; CAMINO REAL HOTEL, CANCÚN, MEXICO, 1975; LA COLORADA HOUSE, VALLE DE BRAVO, MEXICO, 1995.

In the early 1980s, the nationalization of the Mexican banking system destroyed in an instant the ideals that my father lived for. A few years later, as a result of this, he passed away. This experience elicited a profound reaction from me. I understood that my violent attitude would destroy my life and the happiness of my family. I decided to fight for my country even though I lost a lot of my friends. I embarked on a mission to establish Mexico internationally. Again, I was given a unique opportunity, this time by Ricardo Montalbán, to design his home in California and thus be able to celebrate Mexican culture and values abroad. This honest expression of Mexican architecture, free of false pretenses, earned international recognition, and taught me that being "international" is different from being universal. I understood then that Mexican culture plays and important role within universal culture, as reflected for example, by the role that Mexican pre-Columbian art plays within a broader universal context. Once again, I was driven to contribute in my own small way, and with a truly Mexican form of expression, to enhancing universal culture.

Throughout my life I have been very fortunate and have received commissions in different parts of the world such as: the United States, Japan, the United Kingdom, Spain, Costa Rica, El Salvador, Israel, and, recently Egypt.

During the 1980s, I was able to travel around the world studying architecture as part of my role as a member of the Pritzker Prize jury, which enabled me to get to know and spend time with the world's greatest architects. This experience taught me that men need to understand their dimension within a greater context, and that fame and recognition are not the essence of professional life, although they are encouraging milestones in one's journey.

My experience has taught me that good projects are those in which clients are encouraged to participate and contribute to the end result. With true gratitude toward my clients, I have been able to accumulate what a client and close friend of mine describes as my greatest asset: my clients' friendships.

Like my father before me, I have been able to develop my relationship with my son into true friendship. I was surprised to learn that Víctor, the youngest of my six children, wanted to become an architect. Being talented, creative, and brave, he decided not to have a professional relationship with me. Even though we were good friends, Víctor decided against showing me his school projects and at the end of his studies he embarked on a journey throughout the world that led him to work with Fumihiko Maki, Oriol Bohigas, and Leason Pomeroy. Víctor was

ready to begin work with Aldo Rossi when I invited him to collaborate with me and participate in the competition for the Children's Museum in Mexico City.

Víctor and I discussed how he could present this project with his own team of young architects independent of our firm. What followed was an explosive fusion of creativity, young blood, collaboration, and architecture that earned us the first prize in the competition. With profound joy and happiness, and together with Noé and Víctor, I realized one of my most cherished dreams, which was to modernize and transform our firm. Supported by the longstanding experience of our colleagues, we built a team of young architects that opened new roads for Noé and for me.

The outcome is brilliant. I am rejuvenated and filled with energy, and I have discovered a new life filled with freedom and excitement. I continually ask myself: "Should I continue along the proven path that has guaranteed my past success, or should I challenge myself and open new roads to achieve professional maturity with the greatest possible freedom?" I chose the second path, and the 1990s represent the happiest and most liberated years of my life. I delve into new concepts, and experience new forms, materials, and aesthetic solutions. But, more importantly, I feel the

rebirth of a passion: to seek and achieve excellence, not just on a professional level but on an emotional and human level. The end of the twentieth century for me has been filled with enthusiasm and joy.

My age and maturity, in addition to my endless passion and the constant support of Víctor and Noé, have enabled me to face the beginning of this new century with the decision to continue working. I am aware that I have a responsibility to strive until the end of my life, with all my strength and dedication, to create spaces that offer humanity the happiness it deserves. Without the limitless passion of my younger days, but with endless romanticism and the enthusiasm of my professional maturity, and with the true happiness that stems from my collaboration with Víctor, I plan to continue working. As the German master Walter Gropius once said, "Work and live as if you were going to live eternally; your ideals are worth it." Someone, in this particular case my son Víctor, will take those ideals and continue along this road, which Villagrán once described as not being long, but endless.

RICARDO LEGORRETA
Mexico, February 2003

PAPALOTE CHILDREN'S MUSEUM, MEXICO CITY, MEXICO, 1994.

I have lived surrounded by architecture. When I was a child, family trips inevitably included visiting the sites of great buildings and cities. The home I grew up in as a child had an extensive collection of architecture books and was constantly being remodeled. Although I was uncertain that I could have a successful professional relationship with my father, I always knew that my greatest dream was to become an architect.

Architecture today can be distinguished from other art forms because it thrives on collaboration and team effort. This distinction is more compelling given that the most successful architecture firms throughout the world today work in a collaborative environment. However, this does not mean that a professional relationship in an artistic profession like architecture ceases to be complex, especially when the artists are members of different generations, and even more so, when they are a father and son team.

However, when I reflect upon what makes Legorreta + Legorreta successful, the first thing that comes to mind is the youth and energy of our team. And I realize that my father is the youngest of all: he is living proof that being young at heart is about attitude and not about age.

When you share the same ideals, factors such as age, gender or nationality are not significant. In fact, such differences only contribute to richer relationships and better results in the workplace. The youth of our team is transformed into enthusiasm for our work, it is our willingness to learn new things, it is our ability to accept new challenges and not be afraid of making mistakes, it is our ability to laugh at ourselves and always be optimistic about our future.

For the past ten years, the youngest members of our team at Legorreta + Legorreta, including myself, have had the good fortune to experience architecture from a very different perspective than if we had gone out on our own. We have learned early on that architecture to a large extent serves a social purpose, and that it is important not to be guided by ephemeral fashion, but always to think of our work in the long term.

One of the most important values we have learned throughout this experience has been to love our country and to appreciate and respect our environment. Above all, we have learned that being true to architecture and to ourselves, regardless of our own successes and failures, makes our lives happier.

VÍCTOR LEGORRETA
Mexico, March 2003

THE SPEED AT WHICH WE ARE LIVING TODAY HIGHLIGHTS THE DIFFERENCE BETWEEN GOOD ARCHITECT

1997-2003

URE AND ONE THAT IS TRENDY BUT TRANSITORY. GOOD ARCHITECTURE WITHSTANDS THE TEST OF TIME.

RICARDO LEGORRETA HOUSE

MEXICO CITY | MEXICO | 1997

There is an intrinsic romanticism in our work. For me, architecture that is not romantic does not touch the heart. Although I respect other types of work, I realize that to truly understand our work and what we do, one needs to be a true romantic.

R. L.

N MODERN LIFE, WE ARE CONTINUOUSLY EXPOSED TO STRESS. TO ARRIVE AT A PLACE A
A MOMENT OF PEACE BECOMES THE MOST CREATIVE MOMENT OF THE DAY. THOSE MOMENTS A

ND FIND PEACE IS EXTREMELY REWARDING. IF I WORK TWELVE TO FOURTEEN HOURS, THEN
RE AN ESSENTIAL PART OF MY LIFE. I CANNOT SEPARATE ARCHITECTURE FROM HAPPINESS. **R. L.**

The true beauty in nature, as in human beings, cannot be discovered at once. The same is true for buildings. I enjoy the challenge of discovering them little by little, each time in a slightly different way. To me, architecture without a touch of mystery is not genuine; the same holds true for women.

R. L.

VISUAL ARTS CENTER

SANTA FE | NEW MEXICO | 1999

In recent years, the city of Santa Fe has undergone many changes. The number of museums and galleries has increased to such an extent that Santa Fe has become the third most important artistic center in the United States. The College of Santa Fe understood the need to create a program for the visual arts that would attract the best students and professors in the country and be recognized at a national level as a leader of the arts. To attain this goal, it was necessary to create a unique program of studies, as well as

facilities with an architectural design that would stimulate creativity and promote interaction among students from diverse backgrounds.

The first stage comprises the Santa Fe Art Institute (1,500 square meters), the Photographic Art Center (1,000 square meters) and the Art History and Visual Resources Center (3,500 square meters). At the second stage, the Studio Building dedicated to the plastic arts was included.

The Santa Fe Art Institute includes workshops, offices, and twelve dormitories for students. The Art History and Visual Resources Center houses galleries, meeting rooms, multi-purpose rooms, offices, and an auditorium accommodating 300 people.

The Three-dimensional and Two-dimensional Arts Center includes computer facilities, classrooms, lecture halls, lounges, and offices.

1. Art History and Visual
   Resources Center

2. Santa Fe Art Institute

3. Photographic Art Center

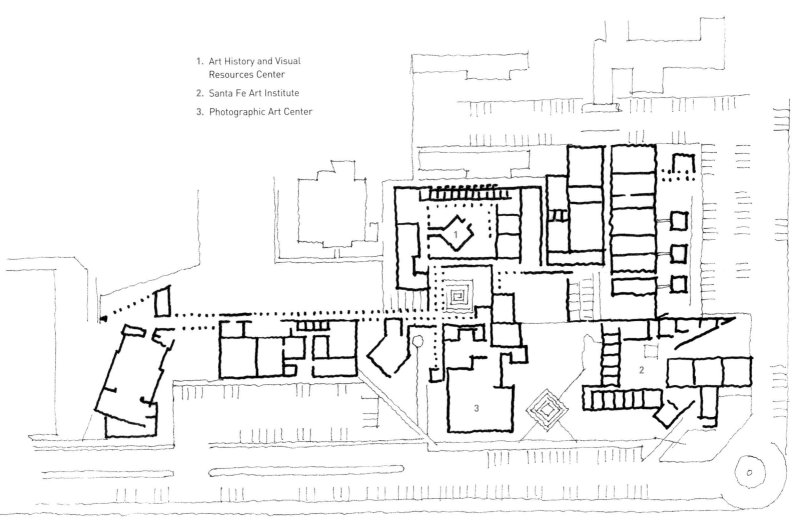

The Life of an Architect

The life of an architect is full of contrasts. During one single day we can move from:

- Dreaming of new projects, to a meeting with contractors to go over a given budget and schedule.

- Figuring out how to make projects trans- cendent, to achieving a new functional approach for a building.

- Dealing with the owner of a luxury house, to talking with a bricklayer about stuccowork.

- Designing a compound for a university campus, to designing a doorknob.

- Imagining the perfect project, to inspecting a built work and noticing all the things we could have done better.

- Being distressed from lack of work, to being overwhelmed by the amount of urgent projects to cope with.

- Discussing a work of art with its author, to discussing a building's structure with the engineers.

- Designing buildings to withstand many years, to planning the remodeling of an office building into new usage.

The life of an architect is neither that of an entrepreneur nor that of an artist. It is full of contrasts, and the architect must find in that circumstance not frustration, but opportunities to stimulate creativity.

V.L.

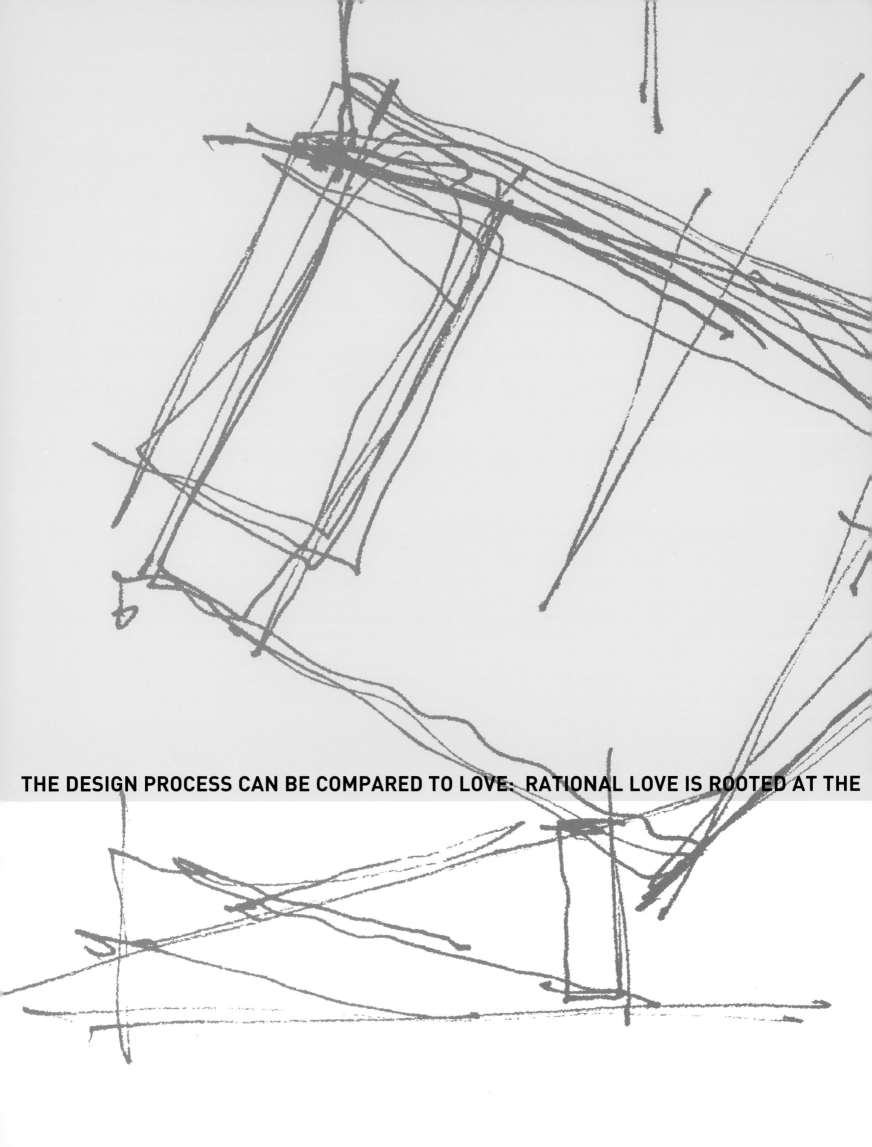

THE DESIGN PROCESS CAN BE COMPARED TO LOVE: RATIONAL LOVE IS ROOTED AT THE

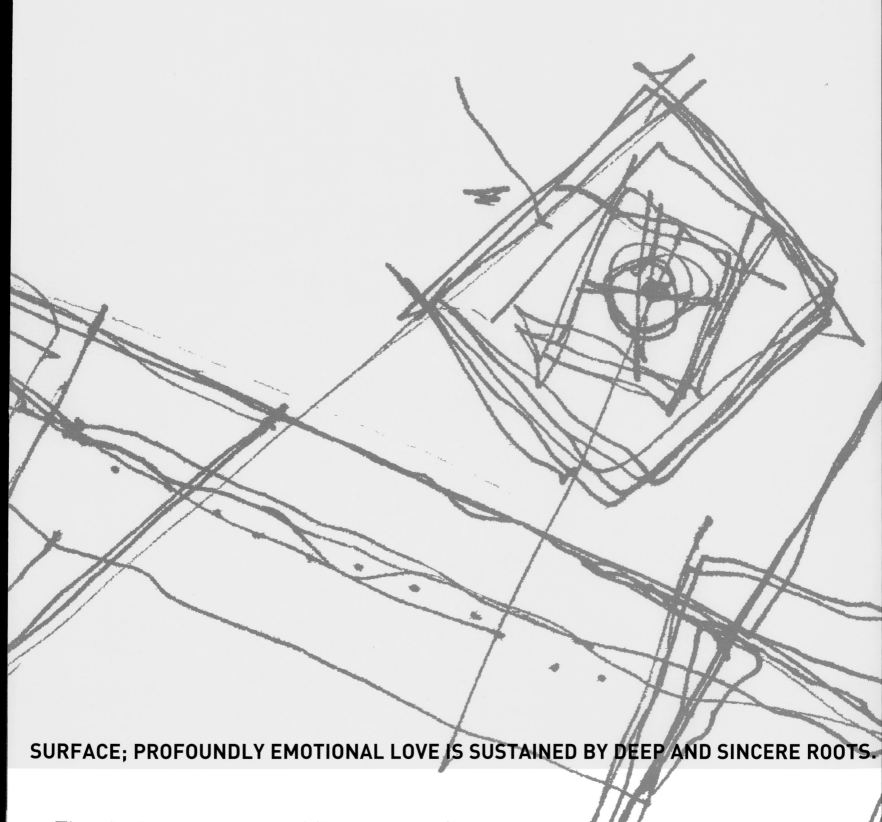

SURFACE; PROFOUNDLY EMOTIONAL LOVE IS SUSTAINED BY DEEP AND SINCERE ROOTS.

The design process and its spontaneity are driven by the emotions of the designer and invite observers to let loose their imagination. When I dream, I dream about those architectural and Mexican elements such as color, walls, mystery and intimacy that attract me the most.

R. L.

THE CONSTRUCTION PROCESS CAN BE PAINFUL TO SOME, BUT PLEASURABLE TO
TO BUILD. A TRUE ARCHITECT GOES BEYOND THE DRAWING TABLE AND INTO THE
TOOLS, NOT ENDS IN THEMSELVES. I CAN'T IMAGINE AN ARCHITECT WHO DOES N

It is dangerous to design without specifications. To do "whatever you want" represents a great risk because architecture, unlike other art forms, is a solution to a problem. If we lose sight of this functional element of architecture, then, to certain extent, architecture ceases to exist.

OTHERS. TO BE AN ARCHITECT, YOU NEED TO ENJOY AND UNDERSTAND HOW BUILDING SITE. ARCHITECTURE IS ABOUT BUILDING; BLUEPRINTS ARE MERE OT BUILD OR GET EXCITED ABOUT A FOUNDATION, A WALL, A SLAB OR A BEAM.

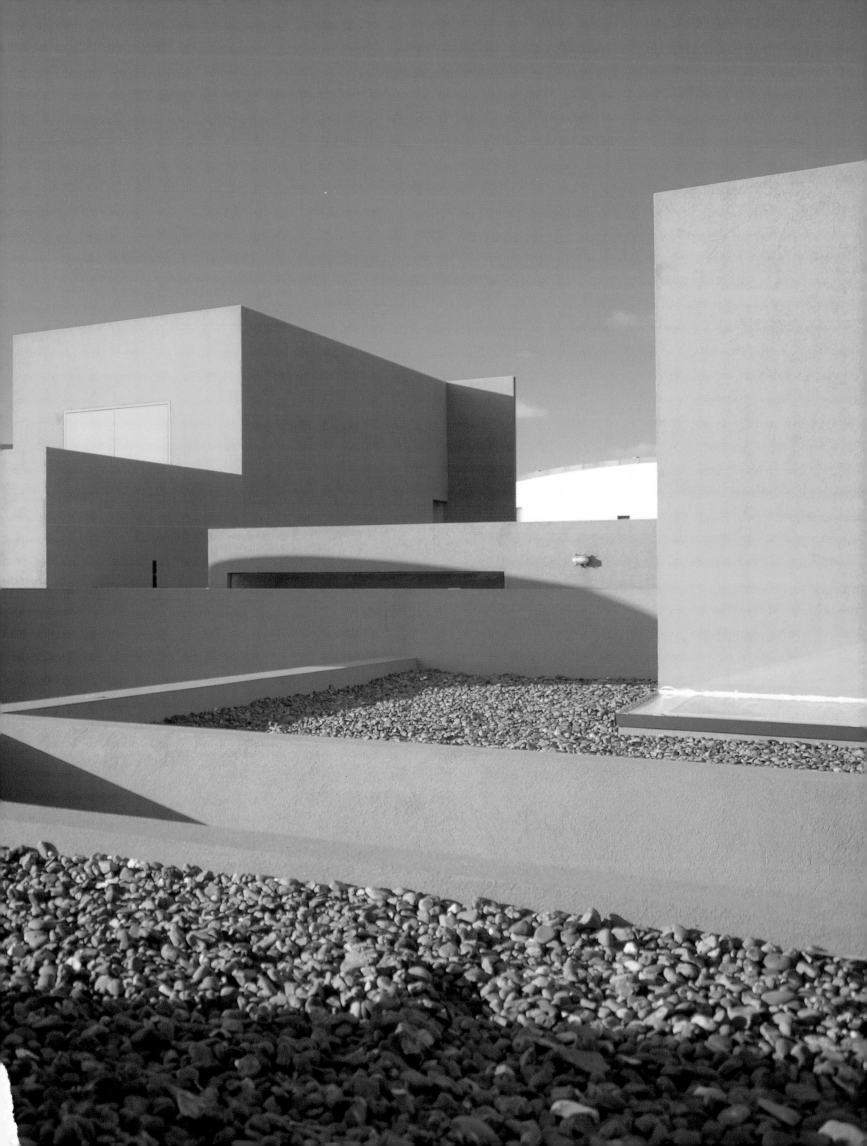

HOUSE IN ISRAEL

SHFAIM | ISRAEL | 2001

The site's imposing character derives from its location on a cliff by the sea, north of Tel Aviv. The soil is made up of deep red sand. The objective was to adapt the house to the surrounding environment and climate.

Family life revolves around a central blue patio that can also function as a fountain, creating a refreshing interior retreat. Electrically controlled windows provide a true interaction between interior and exterior whenever weather conditions allow it.

Intermittent windows frame magnificent views. One window in particular provides a view of the patio, the main hall, and the sea. At the far end of the patio, is the living room, with vistas beyond the patio to the sea.

Each space has its own character: the living room focuses on the swimming pool; the cylindrical dining room features a cactus garden; the children's bedrooms each have their own yard; and the main bedroom on the second level enjoys the best views. Also on the second level is a small studio and a gym with access to a terrace and its view of the sea.

Outer walls are painted the colors of terra-cotta and jacaranda. The result is an abstract composition of walls, towers, and pavilions that complement the landscape of sand, the wild vegetation of the coast, and the surrounding olive trees.

LEGORRETA'S ARCHITECTURE

Ricardo Legorreta is a great modern architect, inve His architecture is deeply rooted in Mexico's timele temples with their solid platforms, stepping pyrami of the great Luis Barragan and the wealth of conte is an exquisite eye and pleasure in everything beau pre-Columbian treasures.

There is a sculpted playfulness in Legorreta's archi tion, scale, dimension, texture, and color. His mast architectural compositions. Timeless and modern, pierced occasionally by regular cuts enclosing both

I particularly love Legorreta's use of a vivid pink, se Mexico. Carefully sited and integrated in the topogr his buildings appear to evolve from the ground and nature. Nature is ever present in a powerful partne

Legorreta's architecture embraces both serenity an from the rigor of daily life, but also reflect the wond Legorreta's vibrant walls with the noise of the sea i view unfolding before you is an unbelievably satisfyi

Legorreta's colorful, platonic forms use water, eart are both ephemeral and mysterious, solid and real. about the poetry of silence and light. There is a beg architecture that reflects the deeply rooted culture

sting his work with a warm and open humanism.
ss culture, from the magnificent, proud Mayan
ds, and walled-in courtyards, right up to the work
mporary Mexican culture. The key to his architecture
tiful, from local artifacts bought in the market to

tecture. His walls are magnificent in their propor-
ery of color is striking, an integral feature of his
his simple, solid planes of primary colors are
internal and external space.

t off by the sun and the tough tropical nature of
aphy and the morphology of their neighborhoods,
yet also stand out in contrast to the surrounding
rship between the built and the natural.

d vitality. His buildings offer a sense of protection
erful, maddening crowds. To stand next to one of
n the background and a carefully orchestrated
ng experience — a moment of undistilled peace.

h, and sun to link the present with the past, and
His buildings, like all enduring architecture, are
uiling simplicity and human warmth in his
of this great but modest man.

Richard Rogers

HOUSE IN FORT LAUDERDALE

FORT LAUDERDALE | FLORIDA | 2002

Located between the beach and an intracoastal waterway, the house was built near the seashore to maximize the view. The swimming pool was located in the backyard to shelter it from the winds and to enliven the garden. The pool was designed with geometrical forms integrated into the architecture and takes advantage of the sites' variation in grade.

The region's intense light provided the inspiration for the array of portals, doors, and windows. The existing legal restrictions for protection against hurricanes were also important in the design. Double height rooms and volumes rotated at 45 degrees produced a variety of interior and exterior environments.

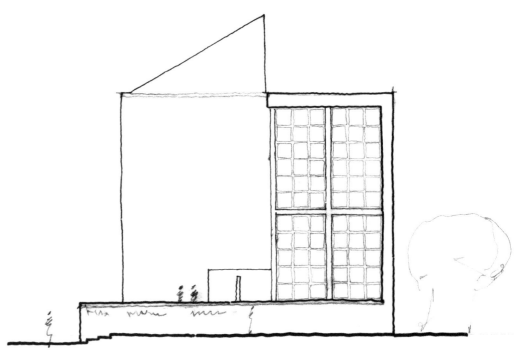

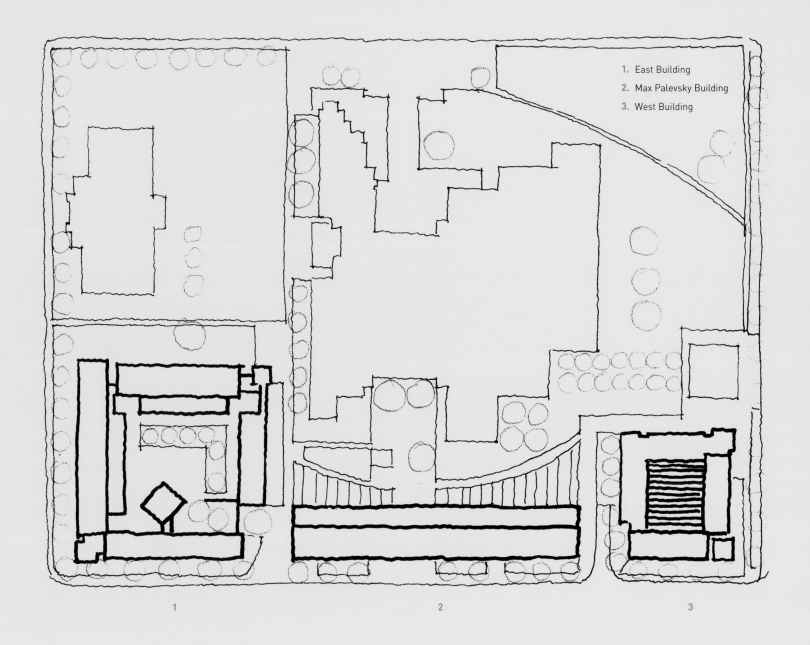

1. East Building
2. Max Palevsky Building
3. West Building

1   2   3

DORMITORIES, UNIVERSITY OF CHICAGO

CHICAGO | ILLINOIS | 2001

The building's design bears a strong relationship to the scale and materials of the built context, while at the same time embodying a contemporary solution.

The program demanded an urban as well as architectural approach. The proposal created an environment around the library by means of patios related in scale to the surrounding buildings. The result is a sequence of open spaces in a variable scale that serve as points of interest on the campus and give the dormitories a unique character.

Each of the program's three main buildings was imbued with a different personality. The first, on the east side, is centered around a main garden. The second one, more elongated, contrasts with the different pavilions of the library, with its main entrance aligned with the street axis. The third building, located on the northwestern side, features a closed atrium housing the main public areas.

The dormitories accommodate 730 students, and contains areas for the faculty.

AS ARCHITECTS WE OWE OUR INTENT TO SOCIETY. OUR PROFESSION EXISTS AS A RESULT OF SOCIETY, NOT TO REALIZE THAT THE ACCOUNTABILITY OF AN ARCHITECT IS NOT TO HIMSELF NOR TO HIS PROFESSION, BU

AS ITS MOTIVATION. THEREFORE, WE SHOULD NEVER FAIL
T TO HIS SOCIETY.

1. Main entrance tower
2. Dean's office
3. Dormitories
4. Library
5. Study room
6. Dining room
7. Patio with palm trees
8. Patio with cypress trees
9. Patio with columns
10. Blue patio

DORMITORIES, STANFORD UNIVERSITY

PALO ALTO | CALIFORNIA | 1997

Located two blocks away from the Business Administration School, the Schwab Residential Center consists of a center for 280 executives and graduate students in business administration. One segment corresponds to the residential area, while the other offers rooms and carrels to study in groups and individually.

Aside from the two buildings, the project features five gardens, one of them adorned with thirty-six palm trees. Besides the bedrooms, the dormitory contains 140 shared kitchens, 5 lounges, 36 study rooms, a dining room for 300 diners, three elevators, 2 laundries, a gym, a computer center, a garden, a sun-bathing area, a swimming pool with a fountain and waterfall, and three parking areas for bikes.

LOS PATIOS I AND II RESIDENTIAL COMPOUND

MEXICO CITY | MEXICO | 1998/2002

Though the houses of Los Patios I and II would be adjacent to one another on small lots, they were intended to look no less interesting than the great Mexican houses of past times.

Located around a central garden, with a fountain as a meeting place to maximize the use of common spaces, each house features a private patio. Rooms were designed to take advantage of optimal view and incorporate natural light and color.

Each patio was designed to create an intimate environment. The walls surrounding the patios are high enough to reinforce the effect of privacy.

High roofs contribute to an impression of generous space in the modest sized houses.

1. Access to Los Patios II
2. Los Patios II model house
3. Los Patios II central patio
4. Access to Los Patios I
5. Paddle tennis court
6. Los Patios I model house
7. Los Patios I main garden

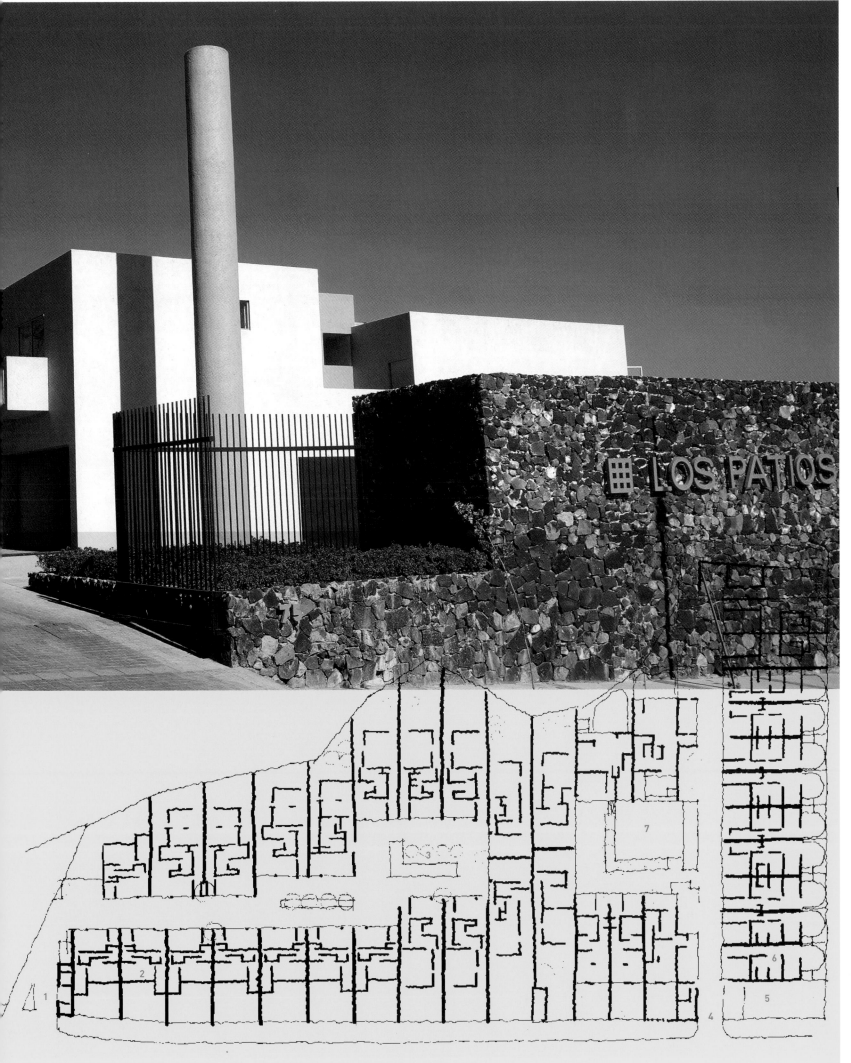

LOS PATIOS

TELMEX TECHNOLOGY CENTER

MEXICO CITY | MEXICO | 2003

Conceived as part of an ambitious urban renewal plan for the
historic center of Mexico City and located in a high quality
structure representative of the architecture of the 1950s,
this technology center creates an attractive setting to showcase
the latest advances in communications technology for residential
and business applications.

The concrete structure and various installations remain
uncovered and visible. This allows the center the flexibility
to create a series of environments or spaces in which to
demonstrate technology solutions for various settings such
as the home, the office, an airport, a security center, etc.

A platform surrounded by viewing screens serves as the center's
entry point. In the short time required to traverse this space,
the screens display the history of communication.

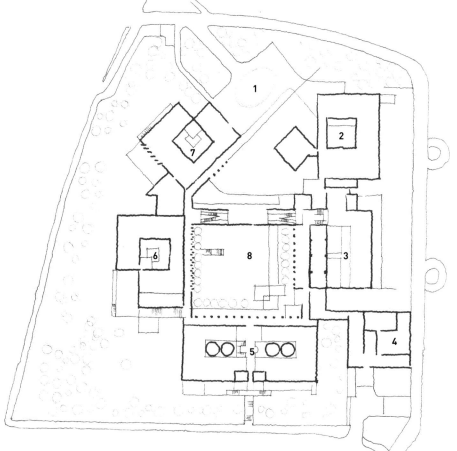

1. Main entrance square
2. Executive office
3. Dining room
4. General services
5. Administration
6. Sales
7. Editorial
8. Central patio

TELEVISA SANTA FE

MEXICO CITY │ MEXICO │ 1998

The complex of buildings that make up Televisa Santa Fe was conceived with great flexibility. The aim was to give an individual character to each building. A plaza allows access for cars and pedestrians. The 46,000-square-meter site accommodates five four-level buildings connected to each other by portals. A dome-shaped roof connects each building hall to elevators, stairs, restrooms, and other service areas.

Each building has its own character in shape and proportions, granting a great flexibility to the whole while providing a particular look and feel to each area individually. This allows the buildings to function as a great corporate headquarters or as a compound for multiple enterprises without losing their character.

The office areas were designed to take advantage of natural light, and feature open, tree-filled gardens in addition to the expected complement state-of-the-art telecommunication technologies.

The design grants elegance, humanism, and efficiency to each building, creating a friendly working environment.

The three-level parking area in the basement has a capacity for 1,860 vehicles and is high enough to permit natural light to filter through, eliminating the sensation of enclosure common to such areas.

STAIRS ARE ADVENTUROUS. THEY INDICATE A PATH, BUT NOT ALWAYS A DESTINATION. YET, THEY ENABLE US TO PLAY WITH COLOR, LIGHT, MYSTERY, AND MOVEMENT.

LOMAS HOUSE

MEXICO CITY | MEXICO | 2001

Due to the close proximity of a commercial center, the various spaces in this house are oriented to the interior, with virtually no relationship with the surrounding environments.

Official regulations dictating a separation between adjacent areas were used to generate breathing zones and perimeter transitions throughout the project.

The house is distributed among three floors. Most of the service areas are located in the basement, while the upper floor houses the bedrooms and a game room. The upper floor is a place for social activities, and contains the living room, the dining room, the kitchen, the main hall and a roofed terrace. Because it is the sole connection between interior and exterior, the terrace, with a fountain that also functions as a Jacuzzi, is one of the most high-traffic areas of the house. A column in the shape of a cross emerges from the fountain to support a roof, responding to both aesthetic and functional concerns within the project.

Each facade was developed taking into consideration interior spaces, orientation, and aesthetics. The result is a series of solids and voids that gives proportion and volume to the environment of the house.

LEGORRETA'S UNIVERSE

I first visited Mexico thirty-five years ago, when I was teaching at Harvard University. I had been invited by a friend at Columbia to join him and his students during the university's winter break. Among the many towns, buildings, and ruins we visited then, the most impressive place for me was the ruins of Monte Albán in Oaxaca. In an interview with John V. Mutlow, Ricardo Legorreta cites Monte Albán as the single work of precolonial or pre-Columbian architecture in Mexico that has had the greatest influence on him, saying that he loves it especially at sunset, when it is mysterious and sublime.

As it happens, the sun was setting when I visited Monte Albán and lights were starting to come on in the village in the valley around the ruin. Monte Albán was a microcosm cut off from even its surroundings. Its dark stone silhouette seemed to float against the pale blue sky. Based on my own impression of Monte Albán and what Legorreta calls its spirituality, and the evidence of his many works and statements, I believe that Legorreta's goal in architecture has always been to seek to construct a microcosm in the place that is given to him for those who live in or use the buildings he designs. His objective is the same whether the building is a small house or a large public facility, whether the given site is by the sea or in the mountains. The powerful, independent walls, the simple, abstract figures and forms, and the brilliant colors that he has consistently employed can be better understood in that context.

The microcosm that he attempts to create must naturally be a perfect spatial entity. At the same time, it must reach out sympathetically to its surroundings. That is where his humanism lies.

The space within that microcosm is both centripetal and centrifugal in character. For example, soft daylight may fall from above, and visual isolation from the outdoors may heighten the centripetal character of that space. However, when one looks down, one sees an expense of lush greenery in the distance, framed like a painting by a carefully arranged window. Such experiences elicit a powerful emotional response from those who visit Legorreta's buildings.

The vivid colors that are another characteristic of his architecture serve to mediate between those conflicting objectives, that is, between the separation and integration of architecture and the outside world. For example, the brilliant colors of Pershing Square in Los Angeles dematerialize objects and thereby isolate and free them from all other forms and materials of nearby buildings. On the other hand, in the Metropolitan Cathedral in Managua, Nicaragua, which I consider to be one of his masterpieces, the overwhelming volume formed by a concrete exterior wall, the cluster of white domes set above the volume, and the perforated red wall inside are enveloped by soft light at sunset and become one indivisible whole. The colors and forms merge with nature. It is a moment of mysterious and poetic experience and deep emotion.

The architectural historian Paul Frankl identified "room," "ambulatory," and "staircase" as the three spatial elements from which representative works of architecture in the West have historically been formed. A careful examination of Legorreta's architecture shows that he has adopted this architectural vocabulary as his own and has used it freely in the given place and cultural context of each project. It might be said to be the expression of a natural intellectuality born of his acute artistic intuition and profound power of observation.

This volume on the work of Legorreta + Legorreta shows a new direction in the relationship between place and architecture. In the La Cruz House, for example, a more subtle relationship is established between the small house and its lush natural environment.

Victor Legorreta apprenticed for a time at my Tokyo office over ten years ago. I am one of many friends who look forward with anticipation to seeing how the youthfulness of this architect of great talent and sincerity complements the maturity of the father he so respects.

Fumihiko Maki

HOUSE IN BRAZIL

BARRA DO UNA | BRAZIL | 1998

This house was inspired by vernacular elements that are common to Brazil and Mexico: tiled roofs, portals, balconies, terraces and patios, all given a contemporary interpretation.
It was critical that the house's design cater to leisure-oriented lifestyle, allowing informal meetings with friends and family, while at the same time providing an intimate and elegant space to serve as an oasis of isolation from the cosmopolitan life of the city.

The blue walls provide a dramatic contrast to the lush green vegetation of the region. Interiors are simple, usually white. A local red stone was used for the flooring. Common spaces can be opened to the terrace, the swimming pool, and the sea. A small patio in the back of the house allows cross ventilation.

A significant part of the furniture was designed and constructed in Mexico. The selection of materials for these pieces favored the ability to endure the climate and the close proximity of the sea, and to allow simple maintenance.

HOUSE IN JAPAN

TOKYO | JAPAN | 1998

This project was of particular interest because the client was a Japanese musician who shared our admiration for Japanese architecture, both traditional and contemporary. Therefore, cultural interaction became an essential component of the design process.

The house is a retreat by the sea, south of Tokyo, designed to provide tranquility. The goal was to create a very simple architecture to emphasize the beauty of the seaside landscape.

The main entrance, intentionally hidden, is mysterious, a trait shared by Mexican and Japanese traditional architecture. It leads to the access tower, which gives way to a blue arched corridor. The corridor accesses on one side the living room and dining room and on the other side two bedrooms.
Because we designed the interiors, some pieces were shipped from Mexico. The stone used for the floor, wood used for accents, and some other special elements were also produced in Mexico.

Special attention was given to the relationship between exterior and interior by blending the terraces with the internal space and the landscape fluidly. The swimming pool surrounds the house, allowing water to be ever present.

Architectural spaces can inspire the imagination of its inhabitants. It is extremely important that each person is able to experience and enjoy architecture in their own way.

Architects build dreams.

R. L.

Only few moments are as comforting as those spent alone. During this time, our ability to love and imagine reaches its highest potential. Architecture should provide the right environment to enjoy these precious moments.

R. L.

MEXICAN PAVILION FOR EXPO 2000

HANNOVER | GERMANY | 2000

Located in the western corner of the 2000 Hannover World's Fair, the five thematic spaces of the Mexican pavilion generated five architectural volumes linked by circulation systems that created interesting and surprising transitions between environment.

The accumulation of spaces gave way to different patios representing the different Mexican ecosystems: the desert, the sea, and the rainforest.

The pavilion was composed of large translucent boxes featuring movable panels on the facade to create a pageantry of images, light, and color that allowed the various ecosystems to be represented throughout the Pavilion's interior and exterior spaces.

The purity of focus, the careful use of materials, the richness of the colors, textures and light all combined to generate this design that was at once contemporary and Mexican.

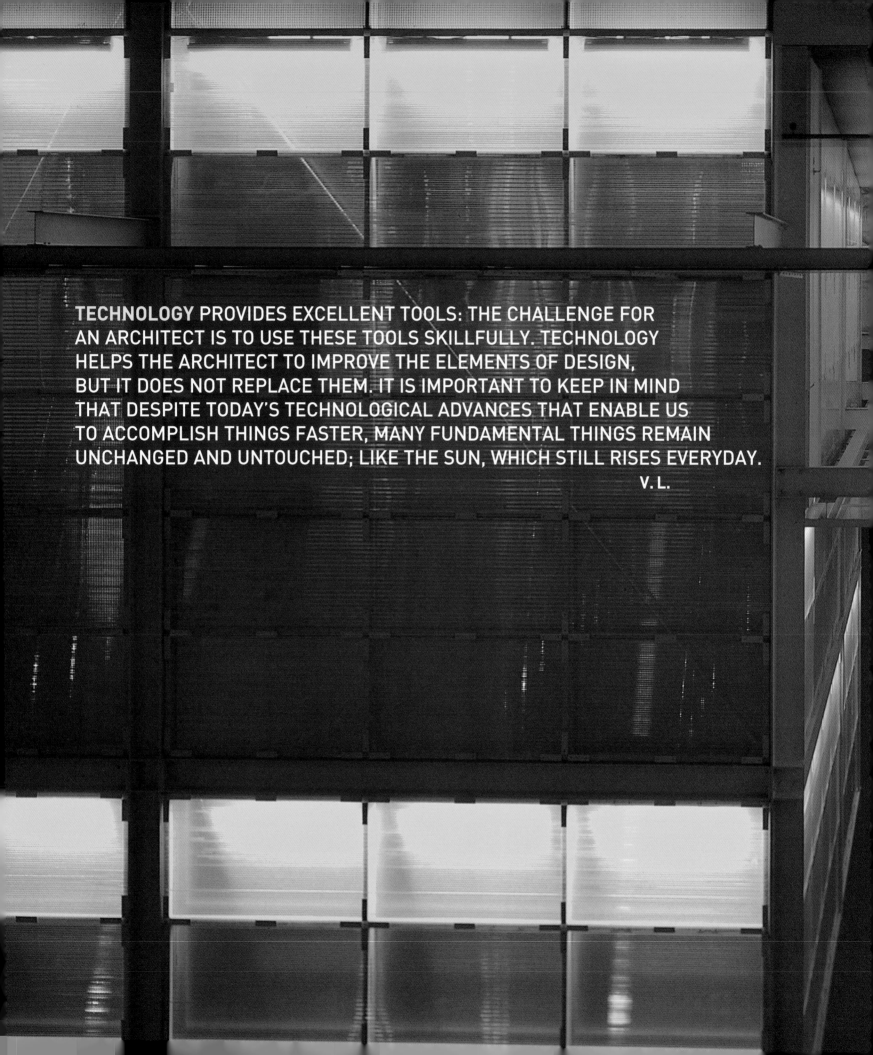

TECHNOLOGY PROVIDES EXCELLENT TOOLS: THE CHALLENGE FOR
AN ARCHITECT IS TO USE THESE TOOLS SKILLFULLY. TECHNOLOGY
HELPS THE ARCHITECT TO IMPROVE THE ELEMENTS OF DESIGN,
BUT IT DOES NOT REPLACE THEM. IT IS IMPORTANT TO KEEP IN MIND
THAT DESPITE TODAY'S TECHNOLOGICAL ADVANCES THAT ENABLE US
TO ACCOMPLISH THINGS FASTER, MANY FUNDAMENTAL THINGS REMAIN
UNCHANGED AND UNTOUCHED; LIKE THE SUN, WHICH STILL RISES EVERYDAY.

V. L.

Francisco Toledo created and donated a work of art representing water in the

desert for the Mexican Pavillion. **R.L.**

ROOM FOR THE MILAN FURNITURE FAIR

MILAN | ITALY | 2002

This commission for an ideal hotel room for the annual
Milan Furniture Fair was issued to ten different architects.
The program required innovative arrangements that could
be put into real practice. The total integration of the bathroom
with the bedroom was achieved by placing a large glass
barrier between the two spaces. An innovative glass shelving
system accommodates the needs of today's traveler.

The use of color and texture contribute to the room's
elegance and offer guests the experience of a new way of
living while traveling.

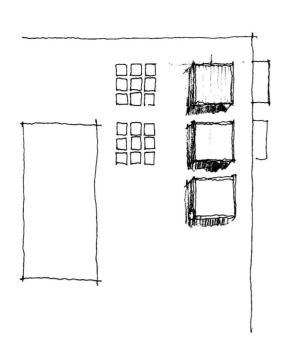

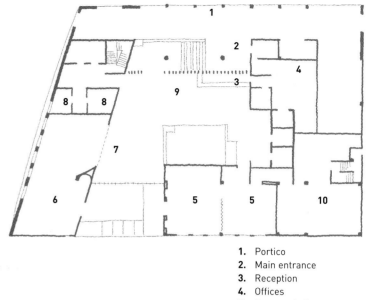

1. Portico
2. Main entrance
3. Reception
4. Offices
5. Banquet hall
6. Bar/Restaurant
7. Shop
8. Restroom
9. Atrium/Lobby
10. Kitchen

SHERATON ABANDOIBARRA HOTEL

BILBAO │ SPAIN │ 2003

This hotel is part of a greater urban project that aims to recover the area near the Bilbao River. The site covers 1,600 square meters and is integrated into the "seam" that blends the old city with the new developments. Urban regulations required that the building be built at the edges of the site. A height restriction was also part of the program. The result was a rectangular volume, inspired by the work of the Basque sculptor Eduardo Chillida, sculpted with perforations of different sizes that illuminate the rooms as well as a central atrium. The building functions as an urban sculpture.

The red color and the interplay of lights in the atrium provide an environment of elegance and intimacy, with the interior design and furniture adhering to the same philosophy.

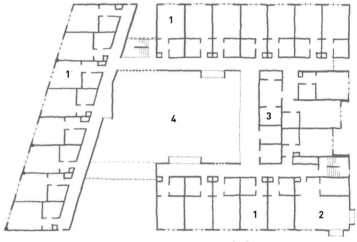

1. Guest rooms
2. Suite
3. Services
4. Atrium

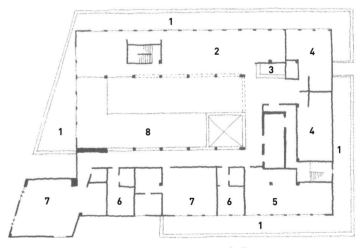

1. Terrace
2. Gym
3. Reception
4. Spa
5. Executive suite
6. Bedroom
7. Presidential suite
8. Swimming Pool

HOUSE OF THE 15 PATIOS

MEXICO CITY | MEXICO | 1998

The project for this house was a very particular challenge for several reasons. It was the second house we had designed for this client. The first house was located in the mountains and this one involved a very different environment.

The house in the mountains was intended to maximize contact with nature, taking advantage of the spectacular views. This house was completely urban with the emphasis on the interior, inspiring us to generate spaces around patios, and isolate them from the turmoil of the city.

Each patio represents a different environment, providing a great variety of styles of living. The patio has access to a series of water platforms, which provide a sense of quiet and comfort. The main hall opens to a patio that may be used as an extension of the house for taking meals in the open.

The renowned Mexican artist Francisco Toledo used red and green Oaxacan soil and desert plants to design the dining room patio.

All bedrooms offer views of different patios and terraces. The interior design as well as the selection of materials conveys a Mexican spirit, urban and contemporary at the sametime.

We had the chance to design the minutest details, and, thanks to good Mexican artisans, many unique designs were possible. Painting and sculpture formed the design's basic foundation and pieces of art were integrated into the design itself.

It is difficult to find a country so well identified with one particular architectural element as Mexico is with the wall. Mexico is a country of architecture without architects, full of mystery, color, sun, and shade, and so deeply identified with the wall that it has become a central element of everyday life. In Mexico, the wall is always at hand, first as a natural element, then as a prevailing and necessary force. In the end, the wall is the most basic element of true Mexican architecture. The wall stands the test of time. Throughout the years, one can witness a discreet and humble wall that never dies: the wall of the vernacular architecture, a glorious wall, a source of endless inspiration. Strong, sweet, romantic, and full of color and light, the wall intimately reveals Mexico as a place open to outside influences, yet deeply rooted in its true character and values. My professional and personal experiences as well as my temperament have intensified my passion for Mexico's vernacular architecture and reinforced my admiration for my country.

R. L.

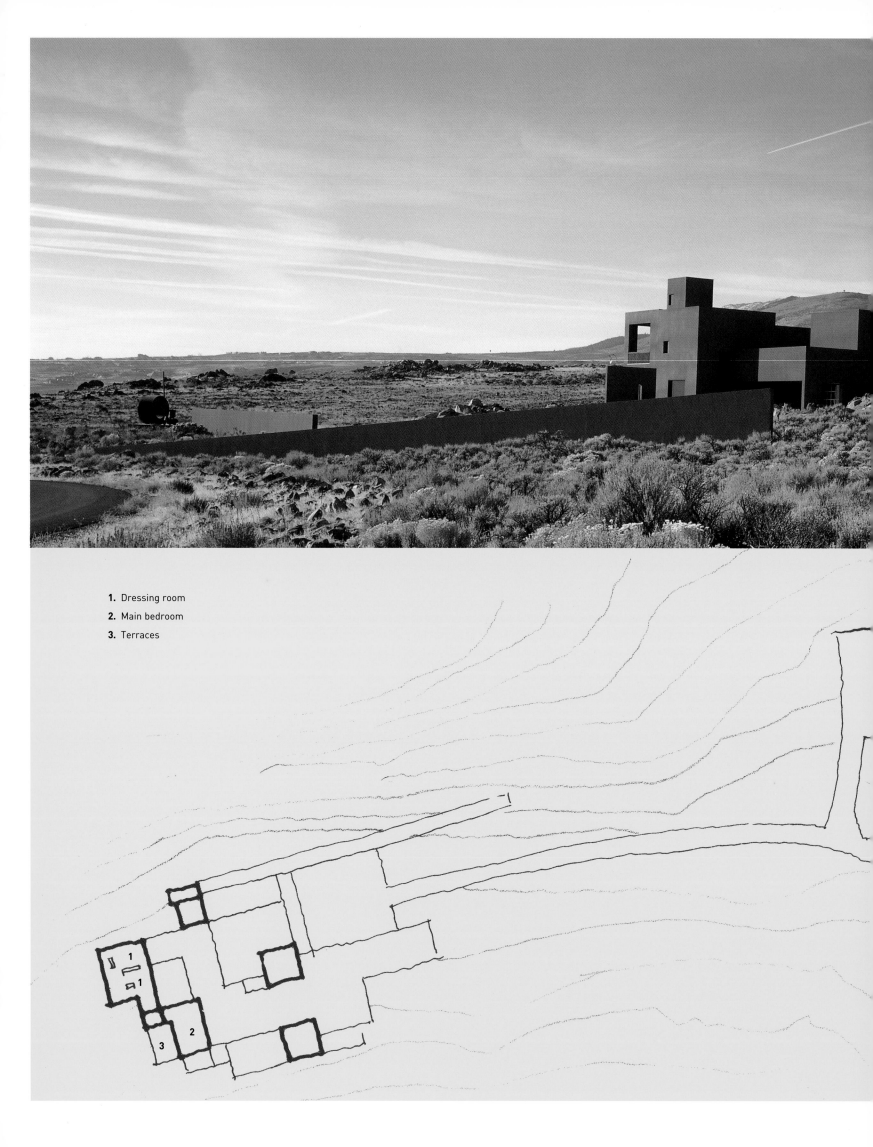

1. Dressing room
2. Main bedroom
3. Terraces

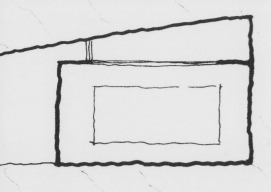

RENO HOUSE

RENO | NEVADA | 1999

The location of this house possesses true monumentality. The mountains dominate the surroundings with the Reno Valley as background. The predominant winds and vegetation consisting of brush that emerges from massive rocks, inspired a very abstract and sculptural design.

The composition is based in a series of walls and towers in colors that are harmonious with the surroundings. These walls and towers, emerging from the center of the site, contribute to the house's privacy and hide the entry from the road. Another series of walls surrounds the tennis court and further conceals the house.

Access is gained from one side, along a large wall enclosing a shooting range. The various rooms are located around a central patio, which is the color of concrete and contains only pieces of sculpture. All of the rooms are located on a single level, with the exception of the main bedroom.

A chapel maintains pride of place: a tower painted in blue on the interior and naturally illuminated by a long and narrow skylight. Throughout the house, windows placed at varying heights, vertical grooves, skylights, and other elements were designed to allow natural light in many different ways. The walls and pavilions were left as clean as possible, in colors that complement the surrounding vegetation. Floors are made of concrete to be neutral in the face of the landscape's power. The furniture is very simple to integrate into the house seamlessly, with the client's modern art collection maintaining a dominating presence.

The surrounding landscape was left as pristine as possible, with only some rocks deployed around the site.

Good architecture has a soul. There are
buildings that whisper softly to us and
inspire us forever. Despite their size, use
or form, there are buildings that bring joy
and spirituality to our lives.

R.L.

TECHNOLOGICAL MUSEUM OF INNOVATION

SAN JOSE | CALIFORNIA | 1998

The structure was conceived as a horizontal block "shaped" by the diversity of events taking place inside. The cylindrical massive IMAX tower, finished with glazed tile, stands over the whole, culminating in a metal dome, which becomes the focal point of the corner.

The facades were designed in correspondence with the urban context. One is supported by the massive joist framing the groove that functions as the main entrance. By contrast, the rest of this facade is a long wall with a series of apertures allowing access to the cafeteria, gift shop, and a terrace leading to the park.

The other facade is more abstract, functioning as the secondary access for groups coming by bus, and therefore less visible. It also provides access to temporary exhibits and to the 300-seat IMAX auditorium.

A spectacular atrium, of great height, presides as the focal point of each side of the hall. The curved wall of the cinema identifies the northside with its richness in texture and color. The southside is very dynamic with two stairs—one to the higher level and the other to the lower level—that cross the atrium from side to side, emphasizing the space's sense of movement, of which the visitor becomes an active participant. A conical dome and a series of smaller square domes above the atrium allow in natural light and create an even more dynamic abstract composition.

HOUSES IN EL TAMARINDO

JALISCO | MEXICO | 2001

These houses are located in a resort in the Pacific coast of Mexico, on a peninsula featuring several beaches of great natural beauty characterized by stunning wild vegetation.

LA CRUZ HOUSE

The challenge of this project was to create a place to live comfortably n the jungle. The aim was to design a house that complemented the surrounding natural environment and was suitable for the local climate, a dwelling place that invited a peaceful way of life.

The main house is located on a hill. The swimming pool and a room for visitors are located on two lower elevations. The central element of the house's design is its cross shape, which is not only a profoundly meaningful symbol, but also allowed us to take advantage of multiple views and cross-ventilation. This shape also allowed us to adapt the project to the landscape's irregularities with the least damage to the surrounding trees.

A hall in the center of the plan functions as a nexus for the different spaces and levels of the house and culminates in a watchtower on the third floor. Each hand of the cross houses the most important elements of family living, always striving for an intimate relationship with nature, particularly the surrounding trees. This idea dominates the shape of the swimming pool and the design of the furniture, tableware, doors, bedsheets, towels, and even stationery.

Each room has a distinctive personality and generates a different environment. The main bedroom is located in the lower level, in close connection with the surrounding foliage. The wooden ceilings of the two rooms located on the upper floor are the major element of their design. An isolated, cylindrical bungalow for visitors stands as an independent structure from the house. The living room, connected to the main terrace and the dining room was designed specifically as a space for the family to spend time together. The sandpit, outfitted with hammocks, is conceived for a more informal and limited group of people. The watchtower provides a 360-degree view of the forest of El Tamarindo and of a wooden platform that gives access to the swimming

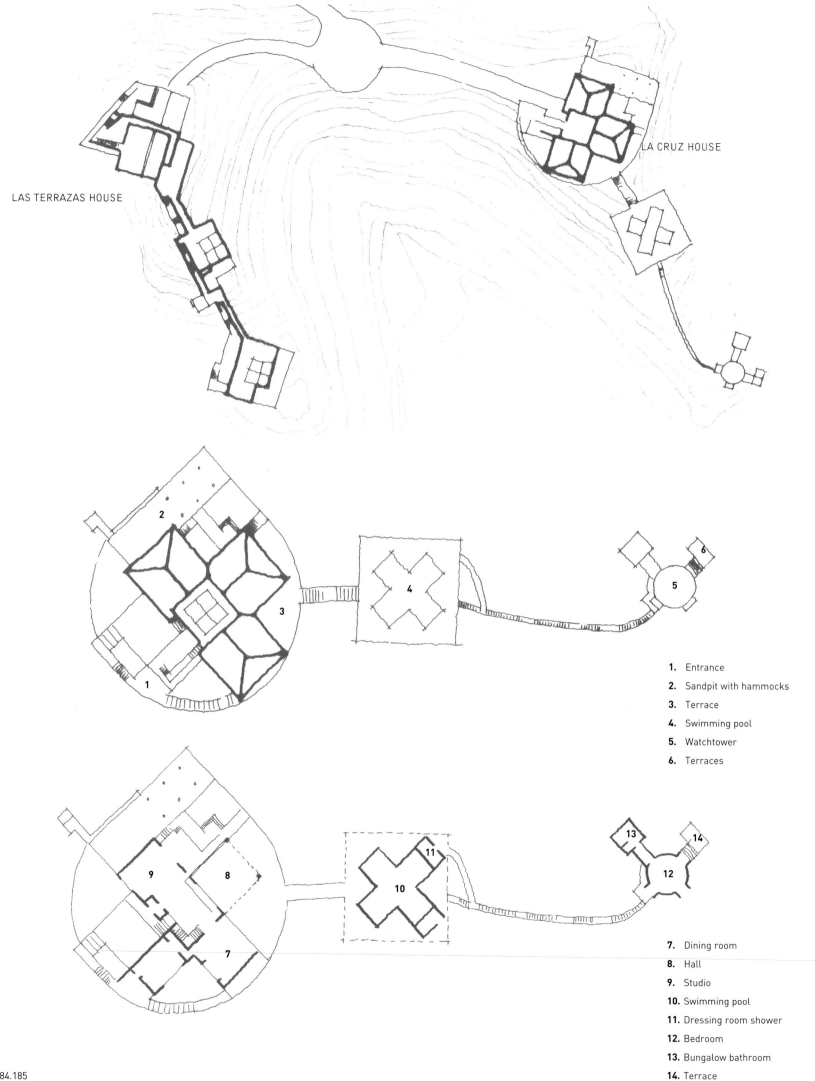

LAS TERRAZAS HOUSE

LA CRUZ HOUSE

1. Entrance
2. Sandpit with hammocks
3. Terrace
4. Swimming pool
5. Watchtower
6. Terraces

7. Dining room
8. Hall
9. Studio
10. Swimming pool
11. Dressing room shower
12. Bedroom
13. Bungalow bathroom
14. Terrace

LANDSCAPING CAN INSPIRE AN INFINITE ARRAY OF EMOTIONS, WHIC

H ARE JUST PART OF THE PLEASURE ONE FEELS WHEN INSIDE A BUILDING.

LAS TERRAZAS HOUSE

The philosophy of this project was to subordinate the architecture to the landscape. For that purpose, elements such as the bedroom, hall, dining room, and others, were distributed to take maximum advantage of the natural grade variations of the terrain, using the roof to contain terraces and a swimming pool. Thus, platforms and walls emerge from the natural landscape offering guests the opportunity to enjoy the splendid views and feel in close contact with the surrounding landscape. The structure's color complements that of the surrounding rocks, and the contrast of sunbathed walls and unglazed apertures becomes the distinctive central element of the design. The compound shows a great deal of personality and demonstrates a deep respect for the site and the natural environment.

WE SHOULD NOT IGNORE NOR OFFEND THE ARCHITECTURAL SETTING; WE
TO BUILD MONUMENTS TO OURSELVES NOR SHOULD IT BE HOSTILE TO ITS

MUST COMPLEMENT AND IMPROVE IT. ARCHITECTURE SHOULD NOT BE USED
ENVIRONMENT; IT OUGHT TO PROVIDE US WITH SOMETHING MEANINGFUL.

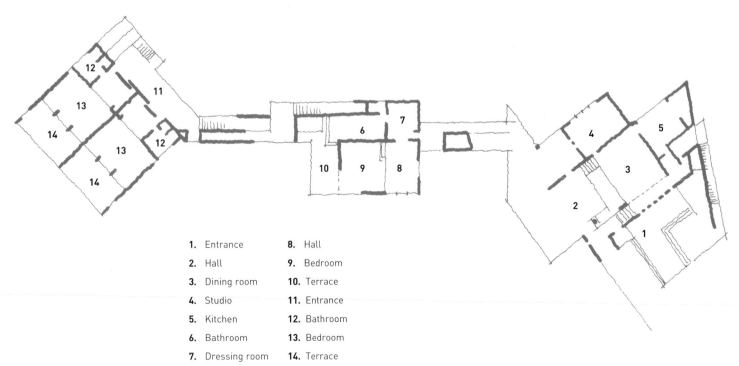

1. Entrance
2. Hall
3. Dining room
4. Studio
5. Kitchen
6. Bathroom
7. Dressing room
8. Hall
9. Bedroom
10. Terrace
11. Entrance
12. Bathroom
13. Bedroom
14. Terrace

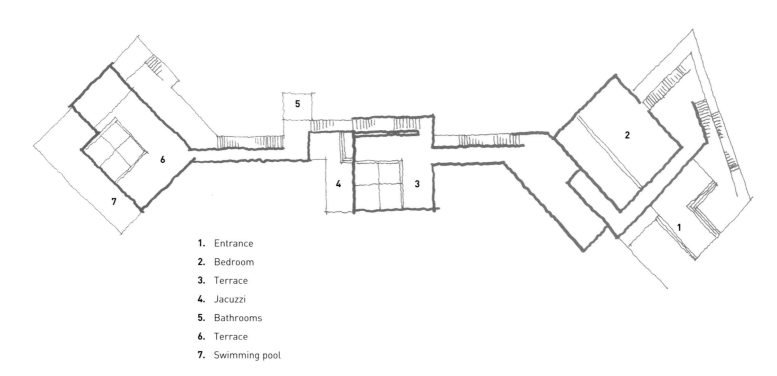

1. Entrance
2. Bedroom
3. Terrace
4. Jacuzzi
5. Bathrooms
6. Terrace
7. Swimming pool

EGADE — BUSINESS ADMINISTRATION GRADUATE SCHOOL

MONTERREY | MEXICO | 2001

This 5,000-square-meter graduate school of business administration is a reflection of the lifestyle of the executives it hosts and while maintaining its essential role as a place for study.

The proposal conceived an ecologically sensitive building that was integrated into its surroundings and energy-efficient. The materials that make up the facade help reduce retained heat in summer and insulate against cold in winter.

The EGADE is the first part of a master plan that will include in a second stage, a convention center, corporate facilities, shops, restaurants, and a hotel.

The structure's spiral form responds to the site's terrain, to the need for isolation from the city, and to the need to create a symbol that stands for a very specific ethos.

Access is located in the center of the spiral, in a 9-meter-high atrium that allows in natural light. There are thirteen classrooms on the ground floor, an auditorium for 300 people, a cafeteria, a meeting room, and other shared areas. The second level houses forty private offices, an open office area, meeting rooms, a library, two labs, and meeting rooms for professors. Administrative offices are located on the third floor. A two-level parking area, in the basement, has capacity for 530 cars.

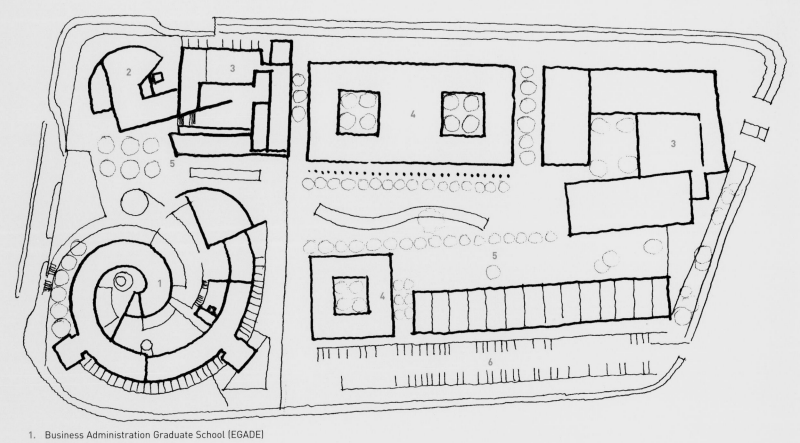

1. Business Administration Graduate School (EGADE)
2. Educative innovation
3. Hotel
4. Rooms
5. Plaza
6. Parking

1. Classrooms
2. Multipurpose room
3. Auditorium
4. Administrative offices
5. Hall
6. Kitchen
7. Cafeteria
8. Restrooms
9. Discussion rooms
10. Plaza

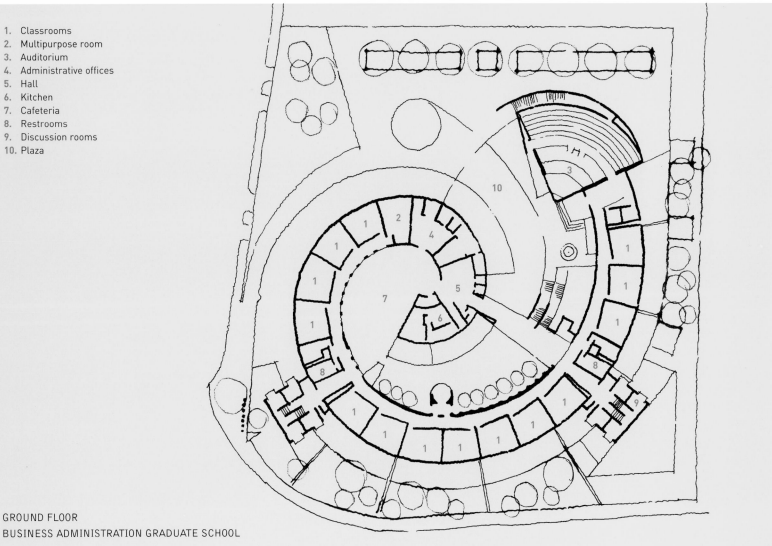

GROUND FLOOR
BUSINESS ADMINISTRATION GRADUATE SCHOOL

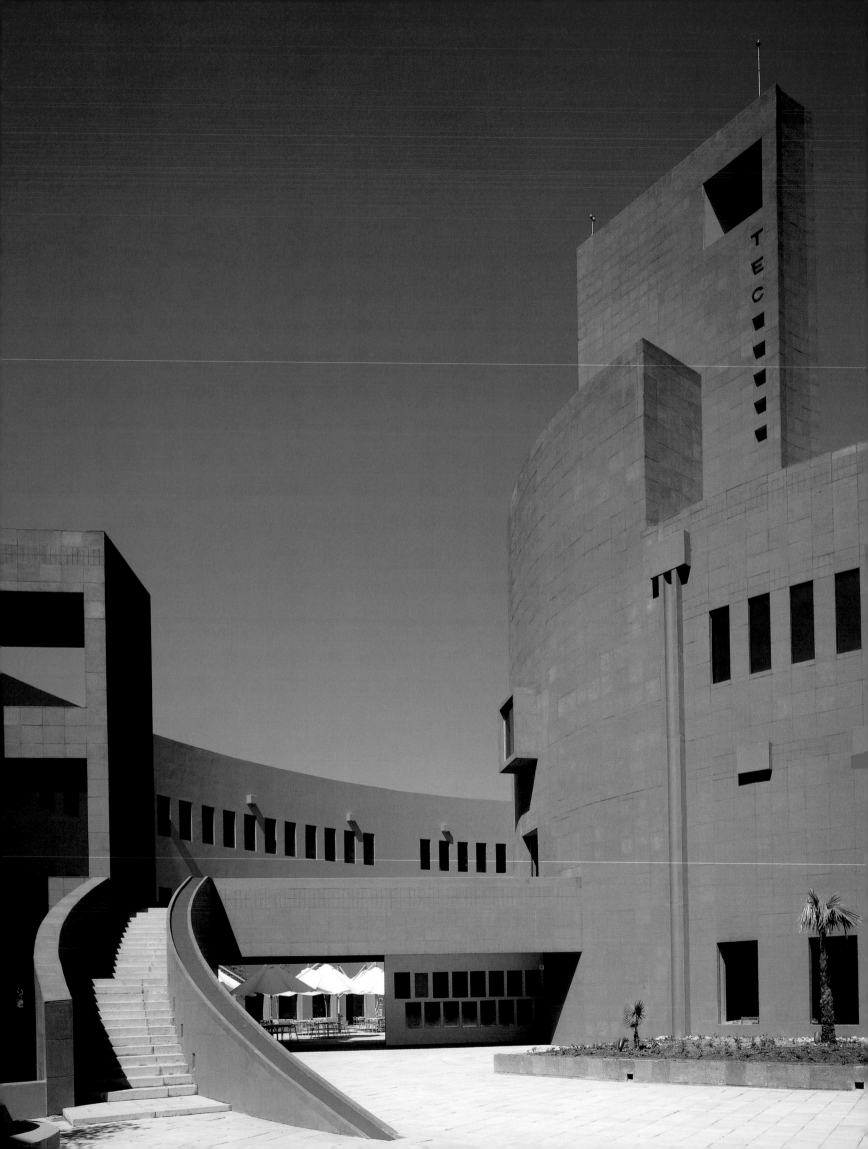

AN ARCHITECT IS THE PRODUCT OF SOCIETY AND CULTURE. NOWADAYS, WE LIVE SURROUNDED BY A CULTURE THAT IS SUPERFICIAL AND TRIVIAL. WE SHOULD RETURN TO STRIVE FOR IDEALS THAT FAVOR EDUCATION AND FOSTER OUR TRADITIONS. I DON'T MEAN JUST IN ARCHITECTURE, BUT IN EVERYTHING WE DO. I TRULY BELIEVE THAT THIS IS THE ONLY POSSIBLE WAY TO LIVE. **R. L.**

EL PAÍS, MAY 17, 2003.

AMERICAN UNIVERSITY IN CAIRO

CAIRO | EGYPT | TO BE COMPLETED 2007

As part of a master plan that involved moving the university's facilities out of the city and into the desert, Legorreta + Legorreta was selected to design the social center and dormitories.

The aim was to create a contemporary architecture with spaces consistent with human scale. The complex has many patios and portals that protect its dwellers from the elements and promote students' interaction.

A variety of forms were incorporated to give personality to each space, which all respect the Egyptian way of life, forming compounds of small groups to foster a sense of family among the students.

Materials and colors respond to the structural systems, the climate, and the desert light.

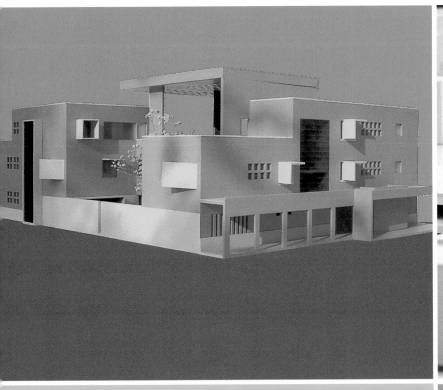

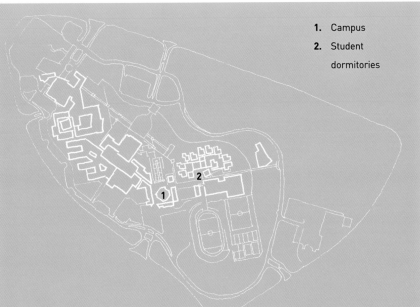

1. Campus
2. Student dormitories

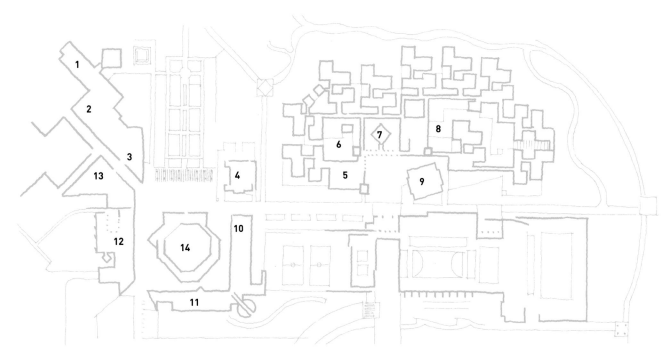

1. Dining room
2. Student union and President's office
3. Snack bar
4. Western pavilion
5. Dormitory administration
6. Men's dormitories
7. Common areas
8. Women's dormitories
9. Apartments for professors
10. Conference rooms and lounges
11. Lecture rooms
12. Infirmary and medical center
13. Student counselors
14. Auditorium

APARTMENT IN MEXICO CITY

MEXICO CITY │ MEXICO │ 2001

This apartment, part of a building with splendid views of the city, is occupied by a couple who have an excellent collection of art and a taste for simplicity of forms. The design's emphasis was to integrate the beauty of the art collection into the architectonic work.

Special elements were incorporated into the design, including an access railing (created by Pilar Climent), a fountain, the doors, and several tables. The furniture was chosen following a principle of neutrality, which was much needed to create an environment of peace and elegance while emphasizing the spectacular views.

HOUSE IN HAWAII

MAUI | HAWAII | 2002

Located in an affluent seaside neighborhood, this house was conceived as a resting and meeting place, taking great advantage of the view of the Pacific Ocean and integrating interior and exterior spaces by means of patios, terraces, balconies, and large windows.

Since the construction was adapted to the natural slope of the site, only a discreet series of volumes may be appreciated from the outside. The main entrance is hidden behind a series of walls leading to a diverse sequence of spaces and sensations.

After descending to an intimate patio and through an access tower, the space opens to a central patio, painted blue. Here, several water features produce sounds that play an important role as a permanent element of the house's design.

The house is situated in two levels. The ground floor contains the living room, the dining room, the game room, the gym, several terraces, and three bedrooms. The key element is a large, double-height, roofed terrace and a swimming pool, an open environment integrated into the surrounding landscape of palm trees and the sea.

Access to the second floor requires movement through a large portal overlooking the central patio with a long skylight framing the stairs. The children's bedrooms are located in this level, along with a suite made up of the main bedroom, an office, and a studio for painting and sculpture.

Exterior spaces encompass architecture and frame its view, light, and proportions. In combination with water, vegetation, and color, they inspire intimacy, surprise, and happiness.

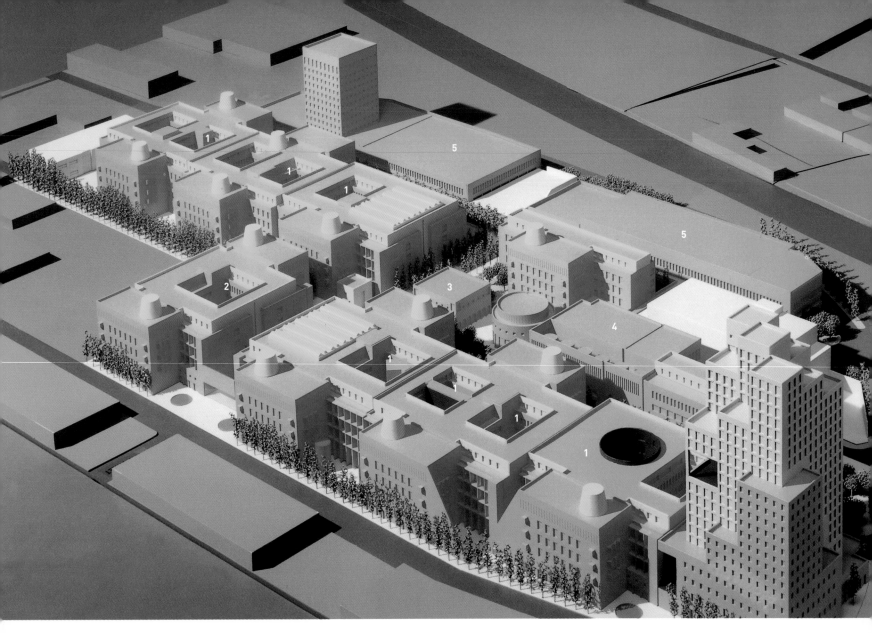

THE MASTER PLAN, INSPIRED BY THE IDEA OF A MONASTERY OR A SCIENTIFIC VILLAGE, LOCATED EAST OF SAN FRANCISCO BAY, WITH 230,000 SQUARE METERS OF CONSTRUCTION TO BE COMPLETED OVER A PERIOD OF FIFTEEN YEARS.

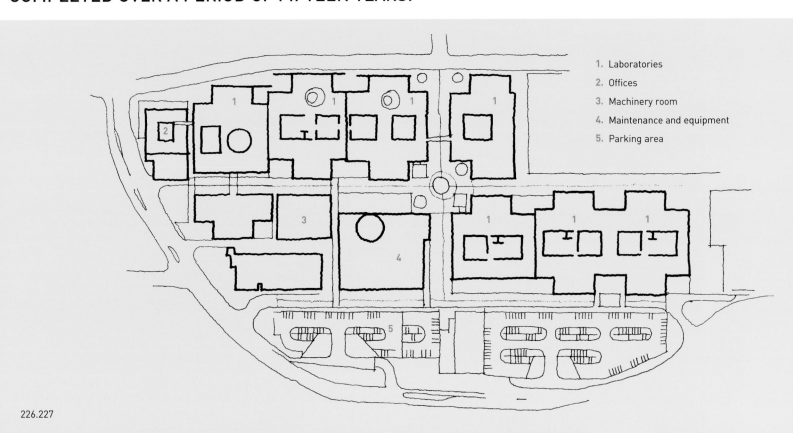

1. Laboratories
2. Offices
3. Machinery room
4. Maintenance and equipment
5. Parking area

CHIRON LIFE AND SCIENCE LABORATORIES

EMERYVILLE | CALIFORNIA | 1999

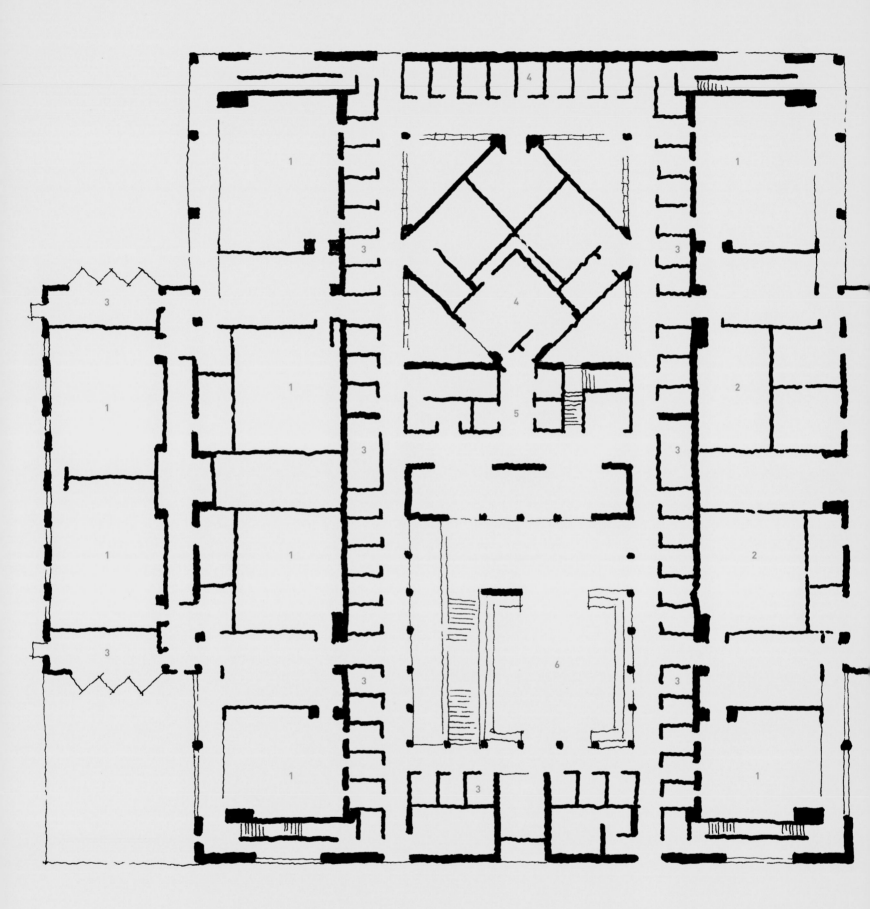

1. Laboratory
2. Equipment
3. Offices
4. Meeting room
5. Services
6. Atrium

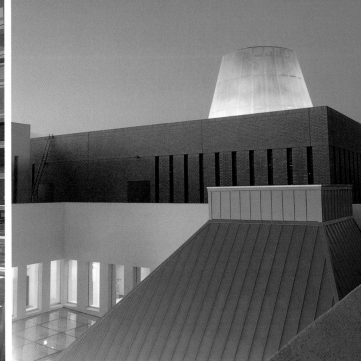

CHIRON LIFE AND SCIENCE LABORATORIES

EMERYVILLE │ CALIFORNIA │ 1999

Located east of San Francisco Bay and 230,000 square meters of built space, Chiron's research facility was conceived to create a stimulating and interactive environment for Chiron's scientists and personnel in a campus characterized by highly distinctive architecture. Chiron, a quickly growing biotechnological research corporation, wanted its facilities to express the vision and success of the company, while at the same time reinforcing its work philosophy and culture. The greatest challenge for this project was to successfully combine an innovative design with a functional program in an environment that supported teamwork and promoted communication between the company's scientists and the rest of the staff.

The master plan was inspired by the idea of a monastery or a scientific village, emulating the order and organization of the small community contained within. The modules for the laboratories were defined by a series of atriums, patios, and plazas, integrated to create a great multilevel campus. Access to the campus maintains a pedestrian scale along several streets that lead to a central plaza. This plaza, which functions as the compound's main entrance, is flanked by two entry pavilions hosting an auditorium and a cafeteria open to the general public.

The main pedestrian walkway on the second level includes a large atrium that represents the total integration of forms, colors, textures, and light. The laboratories for research and the researchers' private rooms are located around the patio. The labs enjoy the use of natural light and views of the bay and the mountains.

The project's initial stage comprises 26,000 square meters of laboratories. The ground floor contains machinery and special areas supporting the laboratories. The three upper levels correspond to the flexible lab areas, which can be adapted to different research needs. A total of 230,000 square meters of construction will be developed over a period of fifteen years.

EL ROBLE OFFICE BUILDING

ESCAZÚ │ COSTA RICA │ 2000

Located in an area with extensive vegetation and high rain levels, the site for this project is part of an existing compound that includes a hotel and a commercial center.

The master plan dictated that the exterior spaces, comprised of plazas and patios, should be integrated with the buildings by means of a portico, which provides a sense of scale and protection from the elements. The plan was divided into two stages: The initial stage focused on the two main office buildings. The first is a four-level building with access through an arched hall into a central patio. The second building has three levels and is surrounded by water. The compound also features a parking area for 400 vehicles.

Local artisans provided stucco- and stonework, while tiles and a single-slope roof respond to the demands of the climate. The management of color and textures was also a critical aspect of the design.

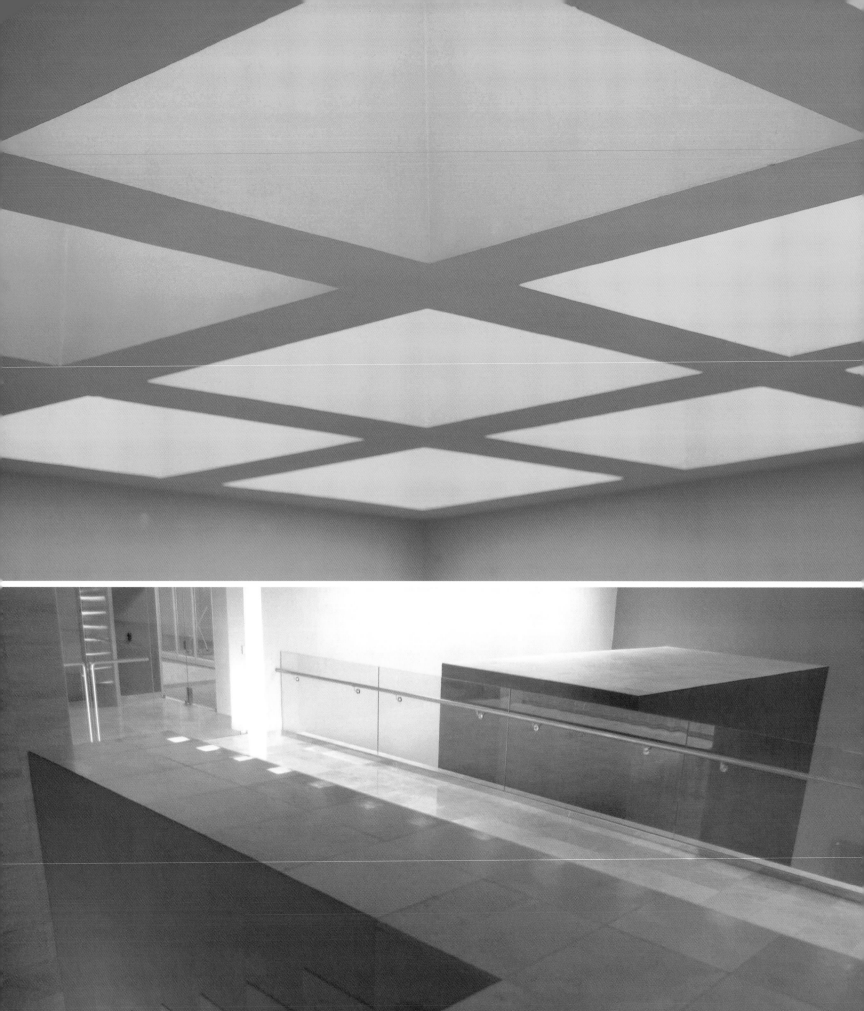

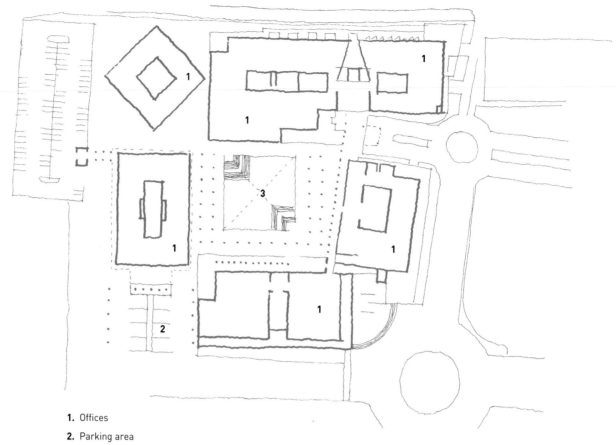

1. Offices

2. Parking area

3. Plaza

DURING MY TRAVELS, I OBSERVE AND LEARN. I'VE BECOME ACCUSTOMED TO STUDYING AND PHOTOG

RAPHING BEAUTY WHERE I SEE IT, NEVER TO COPY IT, BUT RATHER AS A SOURCE OF INSPIRATION.

PARQUE EUROPA, MADRID, SPAIN, TO BE COMPLETED 2004.

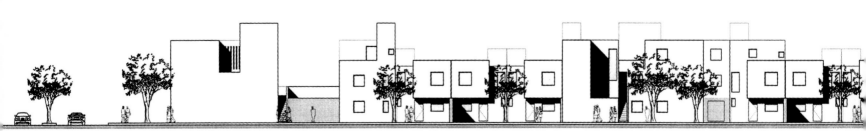

LAS PLAZAS, QUERÉTARO, MEXICO, TO BE COMPLETED 2004.

PUBLIC HOUSING PROJECTS

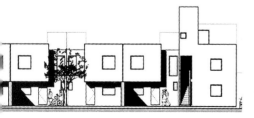

Some years ago we worked on a public housing project, and since then we have maintained the dream of developing more of these projects, which many architects find they must decline for a variety of reasons. At present we are working on two important projects of this kind: one in construction in Madrid, Parque Europa, comprised of 110 houses on a 7,000-square-meter site; and Las Plazas Residential Compound, in Querétaro, Mexico, which is still in the research stages. Las Plazas is conceived as a complex of 242 houses on a 45,000 square-meter site.

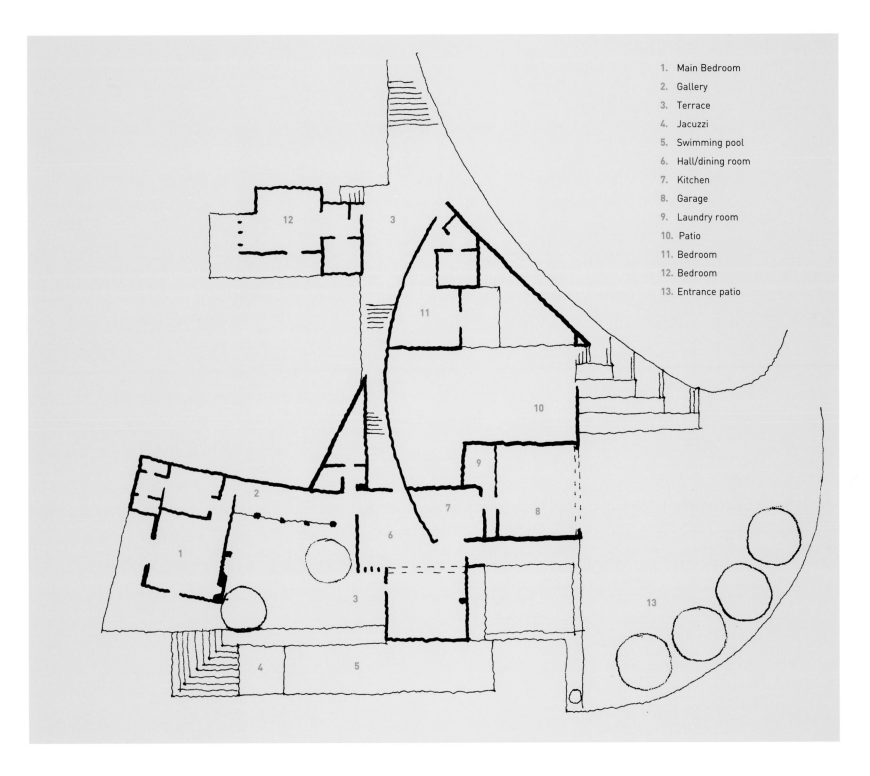

1. Main Bedroom
2. Gallery
3. Terrace
4. Jacuzzi
5. Swimming pool
6. Hall/dining room
7. Kitchen
8. Garage
9. Laundry room
10. Patio
11. Bedroom
12. Bedroom
13. Entrance patio

CABERNET HOUSE

SANTA HELENA | CALIFORNIA | 1999

Located in Napa Valley 300 meters above sea level, this house was conceived as a place of retreat. It faces south to take maximum advantage of the views of the surrounding landscape, which includes twelve acres of vineyards. The house has been designed to adapt to the climate and the existing trees.

The compound is divided into four different pavilions that integrate architecture and nature to create a sensation of intimacy and romanticism throughout.

Family life is centered around a single space containing the living room, dining room, and kitchen. Each of these spaces maintains a distinctive atmosphere and personality through the use of different types of windows and finishes.

Exterior masonry walls complement the red volumes of the house and the carefully studied levels. The intense red of the house's exterior was inspired by the color of the surrounding soil. The house's name alludes to the grapes cultivated in the adjacent vineyards. The total compound is an abstract composition of walls and towers echoing the oak trees that grow around it.

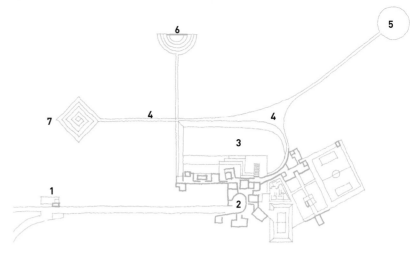

HACIENDA IN SÃO PAULO

SÃO PAULO | BRAZIL | TO BE COMPLETED 2004

Located on an extraordinary orange plantation, the hacienda is intended for the families of four brothers living close to each other. It takes advantage of the site's irregularities, the expansive views, and the temperate climate. The project emphasizes the possibilities of happiness, peace, and shared family life, as well as focusing on the pleasures of walking and enjoying the landscape.

Reading, sports and cinema, important activities in this family, were also critical in the design, as was art in a variety of media. In all its components, the architectural solution here strives to express the best elements of Brazilian family life.

1. Security guard's cabin
2. Main house
3. Garden
4. Walkways
5. Orchard
6. Amphitheater
7. Grass pyramid
8. Bedroom pavilion
9. Living room and art gallery
10. Terrace and swimming pool
11. Patio of the children's pavilion
12. Children's pavilion
13. Soccer field
14. Barbecue pavilion
15. Squash court
16. Tennis court
17. Cinema
18. Guest pavilion
19. Entrance/elliptical rotonda
20. Library
21. Dining room
22. Gym
23. Service area
24. Topiary maze

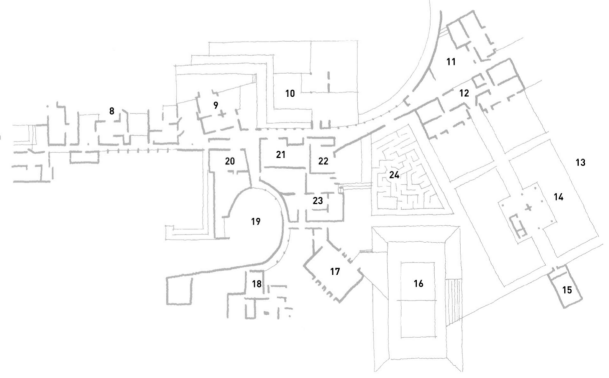

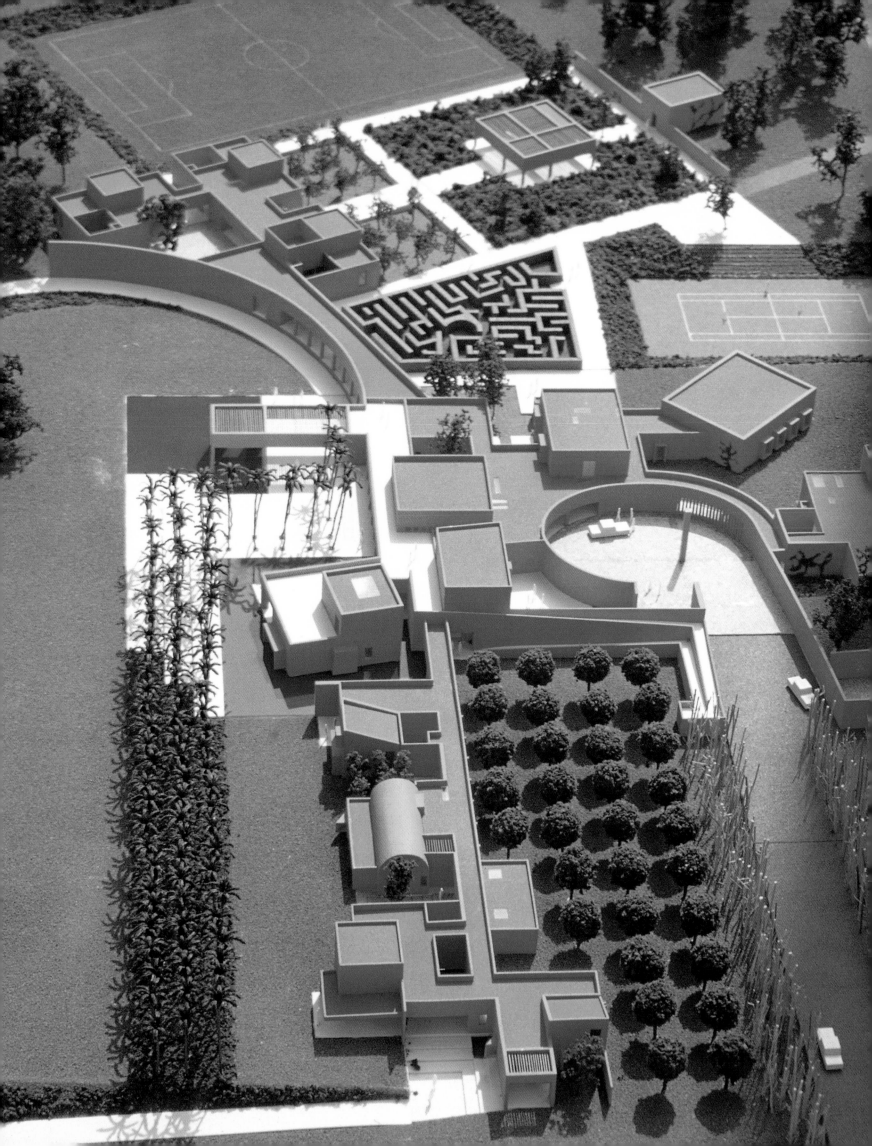

HOUSE NEAR A LAKE

VALLE DE BRAVO | MEXICO | 2002

HOUSE NEAR A LAKE

VALLE DE BRAVO │ MEXICO │ 2002

Faced with a challenging site and a wide range of needs to be considered in the design, we decided to divide the house's volumes into different levels to both maximize views and integrate the walls of the house with the landscape.

Areas of activities were isolated one from each other so that the environment for the older members of the family is separated from that of the younger members. Also, outdoor activities are independent from the rest of the house activities, particularly swimming.

Water from a natural spring was incorporated in the design of the house to establish a strong relationship with a nearby lake, which is a dominant element in the site.

Trees and vegetation also play a significant role in the design, complementing the architecture and providing a balance of sunlight, shadows and color. Overall, the house is remarkably responsive to the environment and fosters a way of living in harmony with nature and its owners.

IT HAS BEEN SAID THAT ONLY HUMAN BEINGS HAVE SOULS. LIFE SHOWS A RICHER TRUTH: THE
CREATED BY MAN ALSO HAVE A SOUL: PAINTINGS, SCULPTURES, BUILDINGS, PLAZAS, STREETS,
MEXICO HAS A SUBLIME SOUL, ONE THAT HAS BEEN MISTREATED TOO MANY TIMES. THIS SOUL

JUÁREZ SQUARE

MEXICO CITY | MEXICO | 2003

This is one of the most satisfying project to be completed by Legorreta + Legorreta: the
revitalization of a 27,000-square-meter city block within the historical center of Mexico City,
facing the landmark park La Alameda.

The 1985 earthquake damaged most of the buildings in the neighborhood, and the block was
abandoned until the authorities began an energetic plan to rescue the whole area in 2002.

The master plan called for a water plaza around Corpus Christi Church, adjacent to La Alameda,
and featuring a monumental 4,500-square-meter fountain designed in collaboration with artist
Vicente Rojo. This solution allows giving importance to the surrounding buildings, a
twenty-seven-floor tower and another one of twenty-five floors.

In front of the church, buildings maintain a height of 12 meters in deference to three existing
buildings.

The complex facilitates pedestrian circulation by generating walkways, small plazas, and
shops that will enliven the area and connect La Alameda, the main avenue, and the plaza with
the streets behind the complex, giving a thrust of energy to urban life in the area.

WHOLE WORLD, ITS ANIMALS, MOUNTAINS, SEAS, AND DESERTS, HAVE A SOUL. THINGS CITIES, AND NATIONS. THERE ARE GOOD SOULS, SUPERIOR SOULS AND SUBLIME SOULS. DESERVES TO BE CHERISHED AND ADMIRED. **R. L.**

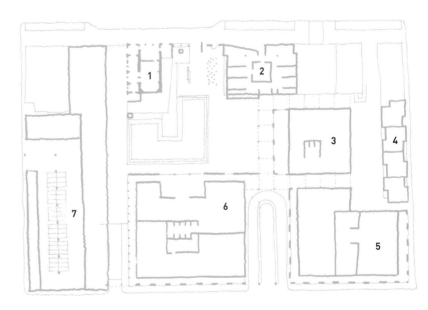

1. Corpus Christi Church

2. Commercial space

3. Offices

4. Residential space

5. Parking area and offices

6. Offices

7. Parking area

VÍCTOR LEGORRETA HOUSE

VALLE DE BRAVO | MEXICO | 2002

This house was designed for two families to share reception spaces, children's rooms, swimming pool, and gardens. Main bedrooms, however, preserve their privacy.

The design responds to a joyful and informal way of life, taking advantage of the excellent climate, which allows a fusion of indoor and outdoor living.

The levels, heights, and shapes of the roofs give movement to the architecture and a distinct personality to each of the structure's volumes.

By keeping the surrounding trees almost intact, nature takes precedence over the architecture, which is integrated seamlessly into the landscape.

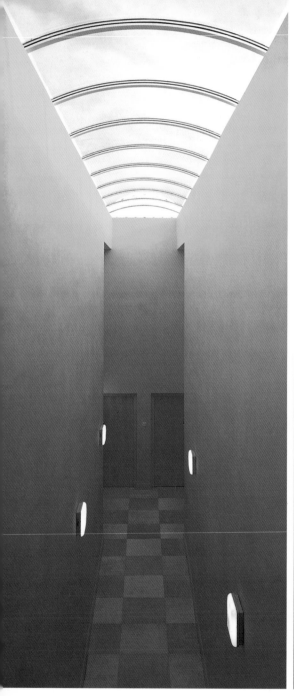

ZANDRA RHODES MUSEUM

BERMONDSEY | ENGLAND | 2001

An industrial building dating from the 1950s was adapted to accommodate the house, museum, and studio of the fashion designer Zandra Rhodes.

The aim was to relate the architecture to Zandra's designs, which is demonstrated by the color of the façade, an explosion of light and energy within the urban context of London, which was very well received by the public.

Interior spaces have been developed in different stages, keeping the philosophy of color and energy and providing possibilities for different uses of space to respond to the dynamic program.

PROJECT FOR THE JOSÉ VASCONCELOS LIBRARY
Collaboration with Richard Rogers Partnership

MEXICO CITY | MEXICO | 2003

Ambient zone

Side view

Ambient zone

Permeable and multi-leveled

Open garden

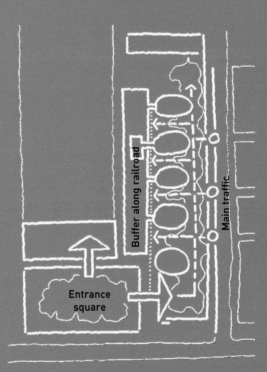

Buffer along railroad

Main traffic

Entrance square

Top view

In response to an official bid to design a public library in one of the oldest and most popular neighborhoods of Mexico city, near the central train station, both offices united to submit a project featuring a building that would be fun, full of joy, and inviting, a symbol of true Mexican character that would also be universal, contemporary, and beyond the grip of architectural fashion.

The proposal includes the construction of a plaza along the avenue that merges with the train station. The entrance hall is designed as a 30-meter-high urban beacon with a half-covered garden connecting to the

The tree as refuge for reading.

Social activities framed by trees.

The tree as inspiration for design solutions.

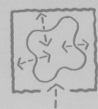

In the traditional concept of a library, knowledge is enclosed in a defensive manner.

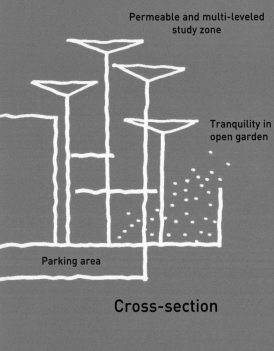

Permeable and multi-leveled
study zone

Tranquility in
open garden

Parking area

Cross-section

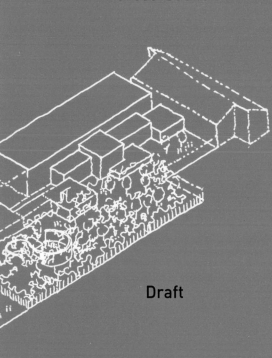

Draft

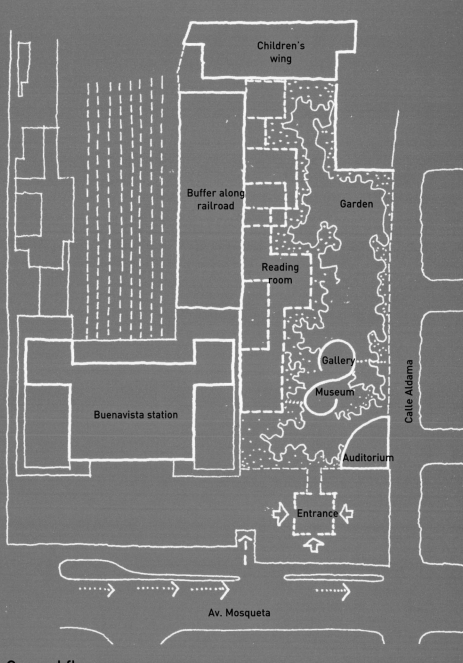

Children's
wing

Buffer along
railroad

Garden

Reading
room

Calle Aldama

Gallery

Museum

Buenavista station

Auditorium

Entrance

Av. Mosqueta

Ground floor

various public areas (auditorium, gallery, museum, and cafeteria). This element also works as a link between the station and the library.

Through the garden, past the security station, are the reading areas, quiet and lush spaces meant to be a refuge for readers. A nearby structure accommodating the stacks also blocks the noise of traffic and protects the open areas from the sun during the day. The site's existing structure is presented as a "ruin" where children's activities take place.

In the 21st century, library, knowledge and space interact in permeable layers of apprenticeship and learning.

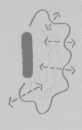

Specific response to the ambient environment.

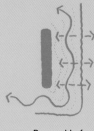

Permeable facades.

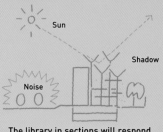

Sun

Shadow

Noise

The library in sections will respond to external environmental conditions.

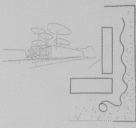

Informal routes through the garden.

ITESM SANTA FE

MEXICO CITY | MEXICO | 2001

The structures were adapted to the site's topography to create green spaces around the compound with panoramic views.

The complex is made up of three main areas: the educational area (containing workshops, library, and academic offices), the services area (containing the cafeteria, executive dining rooms, convention centers, auditoriums, and administrative offices), and the recreation area (containing the football stadium, basketball court, aerobics room, bathrooms, and locker rooms).

The entrance hall has several access and exit aisles granting flexibility of movement in and out of the facilities according to peak hours or specific flow of vehicles or personnel. One access point was devoted to services.

Parking garages are located in the service area, linked by a portico to the rectory, the administrative offices, auditoriums, and the theater. This zone, with its trees, groups of benches, and fountains, functions as the social heart of the compound.

Classrooms are distributed among five buildings, each with five levels, and all with their own yard. Inspired by colonial cloisters, the classroom buildings are intended to encourage daily interaction between students and professors. The buildings are connected by a portico leading to the library, labs, and workshops.

The entire academic area is surrounded by ravines and green areas. The classrooms and the academic offices enjoy views of the ravines.

The goal was to create a contemporary Mexican architecture, where luxury is defined by the quality of the spaces rather than by expensive materials. Ways of maximizing the use of natural ventilation and light were used whenever possible to minimize the use of energy. Materials, structural solutions, and installations were all selected with the aim of achieving maximum efficiency with a minimum of maintenance.

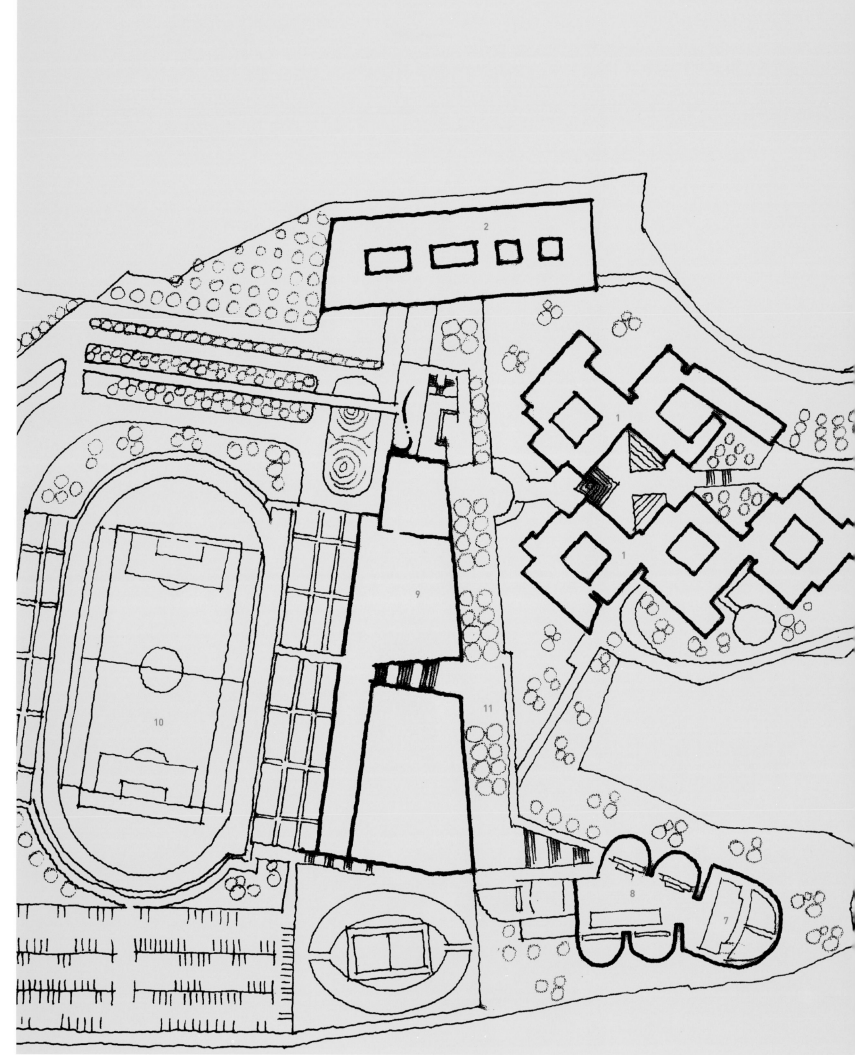

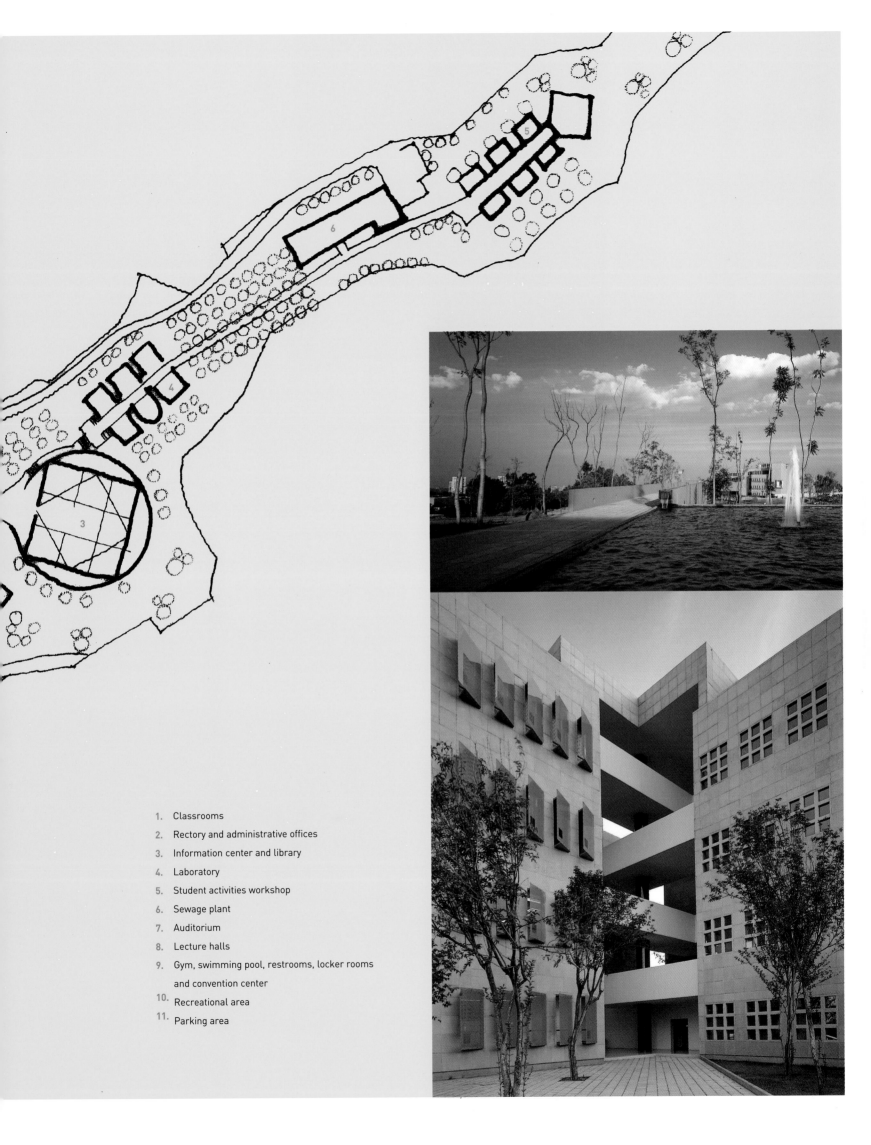

1. Classrooms
2. Rectory and administrative offices
3. Information center and library
4. Laboratory
5. Student activities workshop
6. Sewage plant
7. Auditorium
8. Lecture halls
9. Gym, swimming pool, restrooms, locker rooms and convention center
10. Recreational area
11. Parking area

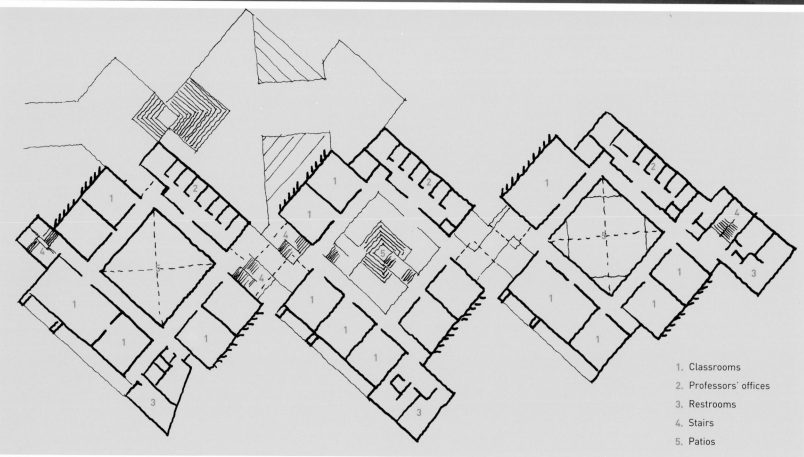

1. Classrooms
2. Professors' offices
3. Restrooms
4. Stairs
5. Patios

THERE IS AN INHERENT CONFLICT BETWEEN CREATIVI

TY AND TIME. CREATIVITY IS ENDLESS, TIME IS LIMITED.

LEGORRETA + LEGORRETA / 2003

PARTNERS

RICARDO LEGORRETA
VÍCTOR LEGORRETA
NOÉ CASTRO
MIGUEL ALMARÁZ
CARLOS VARGAS
ADRIANA CIKLIK

DESIGN TEAM

JUAN CARLOS NOLASCO
VÍCTOR FIGUEROA
JOSE LUIS BARRERA
CUAUHTÉMOC CASILLAS
ALBERTO VIVAR
ROSA CELORIO
EDDY CAMACHO
NOÉ BAEZ
ÓSCAR ISLAS
CARLOS S. BAROJAS
RODRIGO DUCOING
AXEL ESPINOSA
IRENE PEDROZA
PALOMA VERGARA
DAVID FIGUEROA
PATRICIA SIESLER
MAURICIO ORTIZ
MARCO ANTONIO MOSQUEDA
LETICIA GARCÍA
KAREN LEVY
MIGUEL ANGEL AGUILAR
RODRIGO ALONSO
RODRIGO RIVERA
FRANCISCO TOLEDO

INTERIOR DESIGN

KATHERINE MARTÍN
MAYTE MATANZO

PUBLIC RELATIONS

AÑÚ CERVANTES

ADMINISTRATION

MARIANA CREEL
MARU CRESPO
DOLORES LIZÁN
KARLA JUÁREZ
FERNANDA GARCÍA
ALBERTO ALEJANDRE
JOSÉ AGUIRRE
ESTEBAN MARTÍNEZ

SCALE MODELING

ARTURO RODRÍGUEZ
FREDDY LÓPEZ
RAFAEL ARELLANO
JOEL ROJAS

1963
- SF Mexico Facilities,
  Mexico City, Mexico.

1964
- Smith Kline & French
  Laboratories,
  Mexico City, Mexico.
- Automex Facilities,
  Toluca, México.

1966
- Legorreta Arquitectos Offices,
  Mexico City, Mexico.
- Nissan Mexicana Facilities,
  Cuernavaca, México.

1967
- Cedros School,
  Mexico City, Mexico.

1968
- Celanese Mexicana
  (collaboration with Roberto
  Jean), Mexico City, Mexico.
- Camino Real Hotel,
  Mexico City, Mexico.
- Plunket House,
  Mexico City, Mexico.
- Vallarta School,
  Mexico City, Mexico.

1970
- Pedro de Gante School,
  Tulancingo, Mexico.

1972
- Insurgentes Office Building,
  Mexico City, Mexico.
- Hacienda Hotel,
  Cabo San Lucas, Mexico.
- Restoration of the Palacio de Iturbide,
  Mexico City, Mexico.

1963

1979
- Elisa House,
  Valle de Bravo, Mexico.
- La Estadía Master Plan,
  Estado de Mexico, Mexico.

1980
- Lomas Sporting Club ,
  Mexico City, Mexico.

1981
- Westin Brisas Hotel
  (formerly Camino Real),
  Ixtapa, Mexico.

1982
- Jurica Master Plan,
  Querétaro, Mexico.
- Banco Nacional
  de Mexico Offices,
  Monterrey, Mexico.

1984
- House in Bosques de Santa Fe,
  Mexico City, Mexico.

1973
- **House in El Pedregal**, Mexico City, Mexico.
- **Bosques House I**, Mexico City, Mexico.
- **House in Valle de Bravo**, Valle de Bravo, Mexico.

1974
- **IBM Facilities**, Mexico City, Mexico.

1975
- **Kodak Laboratories**, Mexico City, Mexico.
- **IBM Facilities**, Guadalajara, Mexico.
- **Camino Real Hotel**, Cancún, Mexico.

1976
- **Seguros América Office Building**, Mexico City, Mexico.
- **Bosques House II**, Mexico City, Mexico.
- **El Rosario INFONAVIT Public Housing Complex**, Mexico City, Mexico.

1977
- **IBM Technological Center**, Mexico City, Mexico.

1978
- **Remodeling of Las Brisas Hotel**, Acapulco, Mexico.

1988

1985
- **Montalbán House**, Los Angeles, California.
- **Westlake Park Master Plan** (collaboration with Mitchell/Giurgola Barton, Myers and Peter Walker Martha Schwartz), Dallas, Texas.
- **Valle de Bravo Master Plan**, Valle de Bravo, Mexico.
- **Huatulco Master Plan**, Huatulco, Mexico.
- **Renault Facilities**, Gómez Palacio, Mexico.

1987
- **Rancho Santa Fe House**, Santa Fe, California.
- **Banco Nacional de Mexico Offices**, Tlalnepantla, Mexico.
- **FONATUR Visitor's House**, Huatulco, Mexico.

1988
- **Banco de Mexico Office Building**, Mexico City, Mexico.
- **Office Building in Solana**, Dallas, Texas.
- **IBM Buildling in Solana**, Dallas, Texas.

- **House on a Ravine**,
  Mexico City, Mexico.
- **Club Méditerranée**,
  Huatulco, Mexico.

1989
- **Children's Discovery Museum**,
  San Jose, California.

1990
- **Village Center in Solana**,
  Dallas, Texas.
- **Solana Sports Club**,
  Dallas, Texas.
- **Hotel Marriot in Solana**,
  Dallas, Texas.
- **Tustin Commercial Center**,
  Dallas, Texas.

1991
- **MARCO Museum of Contemporary Art**
  Monterrey, Mexico.
- **House in Westwood**,
  Los Angeles, California.
- **Westin Regina Hotel and Condominium (formerly Conrad)**,
  Cancún, Mexico.

1994
- **Master Plan, National Center of the Arts and Research Tower, La Esmeralda School, Library of the Arts**,
  Mexico City, Mexico.
- **Antigua Residential Compound**,
  Mexico City, Mexico.
- **Restoration of the Bankers Club**,
  Mexico City, Mexico.

 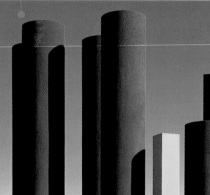  

1989

1995
- **Master Plan and Club House, Hacienda Santana**,
  Valle de Bravo, Mexico.
- **Bancen Office Building**,
  Guadalajara, Mexico.
- **La Colorada House**,
  Valle de Bravo, Mexico.
- **San Antonio Central Library**,
  San Antonio, Texas.

- **Residential Compound Pasaje Santa Fe**,
  Mexico City, Mexico.
- **Chula Vista Library**,
  Chula Vista, California.
- **Office Building in Monterrey**,
  Monterrey, Mexico.

1996
- **Banco AMRO Corporate Offices**,
  Mexico City, Mexico.
- **Víctor Legorreta House**,
  Mexico City, Mexico.
- **Lucía House**,
  Mexico City, Mexico.
- **Lucía House II**,
  Valle de Bravo, Mexico.

1997
- **Schwab Residential Center Stanford University**,
  Palo Alto, California.
- **Ricardo Legorreta House**,
  Mexico City, Mexico.

- **Remodeling of the Chapultepec Zoo**, Mexico City, Mexico.
- **House in Monterrey**, Monterrey, Mexico.
- **Metropolitan Cathedral of Managua**, Managua, Nicaragua.
- **House in Valle de Bravo**, Valle de Bravo, Mexico.

- **Pershing Square**, Los Angeles, California.
- **Library for the Universidad Autónoma de Nuevo León**, Monterrey, Mexico.
- **Las Terrazas Office Building**, San Luis Potosí, Mexico.

- **Plaza Reforma Office Building**, Mexico City, Mexico.
- **ITESM 50 Anniversary House**, Monterrey, Mexico.
- **House in Sonoma**, Sonoma, California.

- **Papalote Children's Museum**, Mexico City, Mexico.
- **Restoration of Colegio de San Ildefonso**, Mexico City, Mexico.
- **House in Los Angeles**, Los Angeles, California.

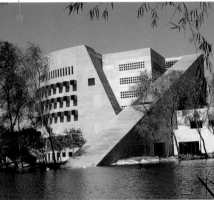
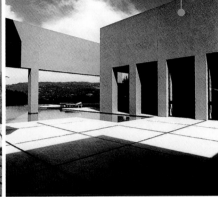
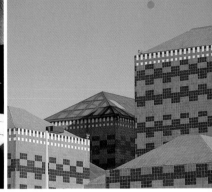

1999

1998
- **Chiron Life and Science Laboratories**, Emeryville City, California.
- **Residence in Southern California**, Beverly Hills, California.
- **House of the 15 Patios**, Mexico City, Mexico.
- **House in Brazil**, Barra do Una, Brazil.

- **Technological Museum of Innovation**, San Jose, California.
- **House in Japan**, Tokyo, Japan.
- **Televisa Santa Fe**, Mexico City, Mexico.
- **Tom Bradley International Center, University of California, Los Angeles** Los Angeles, California.

1999
- **Telepro Office Building**, Mexico City, Mexico.
- **La Florida House**, Mexico City, Mexico.
- **Visual Arts Center, College of Santa Fe** Santa Fe, New Mexico.

- **House in Reno**, Reno, Nevada.
- **Cabernet House**, Santa Helena, California.
- **Los Patios I Residential Compound**, Mexico City, Mexico.

2000

- **Tustin III Commercial Center**,
  Orange County, California.
- **Houses in Hacienda
  Santa Ana**,
  Valle de Bravo, Mexico.
- **El Roble Office Building**,
  Centro Corporativo Escazú,
  San José, Costa Rica.

- **El Fogoncito Restaurant**,
  San José, Costa Rica.
- **Mexican Pavilion,
  Expo 2000**,
  Hannover, Germany.
- **Arizan Office Building**,
  Mexico City, Mexico.

2001

- **House in Israel**,
  Shfaim, Israel.
- **Zandra Rhodes Museum**,
  London, England.
- **La Cruz House**,
  El Tamarindo, Mexico.
- **Las Terrazas House**,
  El Tamarindo, Mexico.

- **Silver House**,
  Los Angeles, California.
- **Business Administration
  Graduate School (EGADE)**,
  Monterrey, Mexico.

2000

2002

- **Tlalpuente House**,
  Mexico City, Mexico.
- **Lomas House**,
  Mexico City, Mexico.
- **Dormitories,
  University of Chicago**,
  Chicago, Illinois.

- **ITESM Santa Fe Campus,
  Tlayacapa**,
  Mexico City, Mexico.
- **Apartment in Mexico City**,
  Mexico City, Mexico.

2002

- **Víctor Legorreta House**,
  Valle de Bravo, Mexico.
- **House in Hawaii**,
  Maui, Hawaii.
- **House in Florida**,
  Miami, Florida.

- **House Near a Lake**,
  Valle de Bravo, Mexico.
- **Los Patios II
  Residential Compound**,
  Mexico City, Mexico.
- **Room for the
  Milan Furniture Fair**
  Milan, Italy.

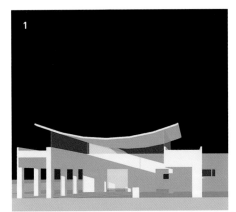

UNDER CONSTRUCTION

Sheraton Abandoibarra Hotel, Bilbao, Spain.
Centro Latino, Dallas, Texas.
House in Santa Fe, Santa Fe, New Mexico.
House in Sotogrande, Sotogrande, Spain.
House in Petaluma, Petaluma, California.
Winery Keller State, California.
House in Kona, Kona, Hawaii.
Grupo Chedraui Offices, Mexico City, Mexico.
Planetarium, Papalote Children's Museum, Mexico City, Mexico.
Campus Center, University of California, San Francisco, California.
Parque Europa, Madrid, Spain.
Hacienda in São Paulo, São Paulo, Brazil.
House in Phoenix, Phoenix, Arizona.
Quinta Eva María House, Managua, Nicaragua.
Corpus Christi Museum, Houston, Texas.

Projects

IN DESIGN

Las Plazas, Querétaro, Mexico.
Remodeling of El Rastro, Mexico City, Mexico.
Juárez Square, Mexico City, Mexico.
House in Bosques de Santa Fe, Mexico City, Mexico.
Camino Real Monterrey, Monterrey, Mexico.
Villas in Tamarindos, Tamarindos, Mexico.
House in Las Arboledas, Mexico City, Mexico.
EGAPP, Monterrey, Mexico.
Multiplaza Compound, El Salvador.
Rancho Zabaco Winery, Petaluma, California.
Thornburg Offices, Santa Fe, New Mexico.
Mexican Museum, San Francisco, California.
Corpus Christi Modern Art Museum (new pavilions), Texas.
American University in Cairo, Cairo Egypt.

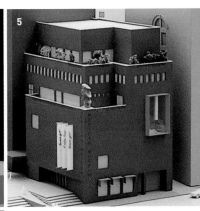

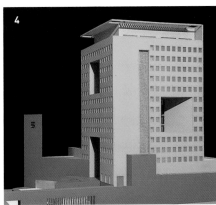

1. House in Kona
2. Campus Center, UCSF
3. Quinta Eva María
4. Camino Real Monterrey
5. Mexican Museum
6. Juárez Square

RICARDO LEGORRETA

Born in Mexico City, on May 7, 1931.

EDUCATION

1948 - 1952   B.A. in Architecture, Universidad Nacional Autónoma de México.

PROFESSIONAL EXPERIENCE

1948 – 1955   Draftsman and chief designer with José Villagrán García.

1955 – 1960   Associated to José Villagrán.

1961 – 1963   Freelance design work.

1963 – 2001   President of Legorreta Arquitectos (now Legorreta + Legorreta).

1977   Founder and President of LA Diseños (furniture and accessories design).

1985   Founder and President of LA Diseños USA.

TEACHING EXPERIENCE

1959 – 1962   Professor at the National School of Architecture, Universidad Nacional Autónoma de México.

1962 – 1964   Chief of Grupo Experimental de la Universidad Nacional Autónoma de México.

1964   Universidad Nacional Autónoma de México identifies Legorreta's studio as official site for students to complete their social service practice.

1969 – 2003   Lecturing at universities throughout Mexico, Canada, Spain, Guatemala, Argentina, Uruguay, Costa Rica, Chile, Japan, Nicaragua, England, Austria, France, Israel, and the United States.

1985 – 1998   Course at the University of California, Los Angeles, in collaboration with Richard Moore.

AWARDS AND RECOGNITIONS

1983   Tau Sigma Delta Gold Medal for Archuitecture and Associated Arts, Santa Fe, New Mexico.

1988   Honorary member of the Mexican Academy of the Arts.

1989   Merit Award, American Society of Landscape Architects.

    Award for most outstanding project in his country (Camino Real Ixtapa Hotel), First Meeting of Latin American Architecture, Santiago, Chile.

1990   Distinguished Member of the International Academy of Architecture, Sofia, Bulgaria.

    Chosen as one of thirty leading architects for the Domino's Architectural Program.

    Silver Medal (for Renault Factory), First Mexican Architectural Biennial.

    Silver Medal (for the Camino Real Ixtapa Hotel), First Mexican Architectural Biennial.

1991   National Award of Arts, Mexico.

    Honor Award, American Institute of Architects, Orange County, California.

    Neocon 9, Chicago Architecture Award, Council of the American Institute of Architects, Illinois.

1992   Architect of the Americas Award, Montevideo, Uruguay.

    Gold Medal (for the Solana Complex, Dallas, Texas), Second Mexican Architectural Biennial.

    Gold Medal and Grand Prize (for the MARCO Museum of Contemporary Art of Monterrey), Mexico.

1993   Emeritus Artist of the National System of Art Makers, Mexico.

1994   Award for Religious Architecture (for the Metropolitan Cathedral of Managua), American Institute of Architecture, Washington, D.C.

1995   Honor Award (for the Chulavista Library, San Diego, California), American Institute of Architects, Washington, D.C.

Asia-Pacific Program Design Award for the MARCO Museum of Contemporary Art of Monterrey, Mexico.

Prize Imagination of the Mind Science Foundation for the San Antonio Public Library, Texas.

1999   Gold Medal, International Union of Architects, Beijing, China.

Honor Award for the Santa Fe Visual Arts Center, New Mexico.

Architecture Award of the Athenaeum Museum (for the Santa Fe Visual Arts Center), Chicago, Illinois.

Exterior Award (for the Santa Fe Visual Arts Center), Associated General Contractors of America.

2000   Gold Plate of the Academy of Achievement, Arizona.

Gold Medal of the American Institute of Architects, Washington, D.C.

2001   "César Balsa" Medal, Tourism Professional Merit, Mexico.

CEMEX 2001 Works Award/First CEMEX Life and Works Award CEMEX.

2002   Presented with the Encomienda de Isabel la Católica, Embassy of Spain in Mexico.

Doctor of Human Letters of the College of Santa Fe, New Mexico.

Distinguished recognition by the Federation and College of Architects for his contribution to Mexican architecture, Cancún, Mexico.

PARTICIPATION IN COUNCILS AND COMMITTEES

1970 - 1981   Member of the International Council of the Museum of Modern Art, New York, New York.

1978   Honorary Member of the Mexican Association of Architects, Mexico.

Honorary Member of the American Institute of Architects.

1989   Member of the International Committee of Jerusalem, Israel.

1992   Member of the Committee of the United Foreign Directives, Harvard University,Cambridge, Massachusetts.

Member of the American Academy of Arts and Science, Cambridge, Massachusetts.

1997   Member of the Academy of Architects of France.

1999   Honorary Member of the Royal Architectural Institue of Canada.

2000   Honorary Member of the Royal Institute of British Architects.

ARCHITECTURAL AWARDS JUROR

1977   Member of the Jury of the American Institute of Architects, Chicago, Illinois.

1983 - 1993   Member of the Pritzker Prize Jury.

1984   Member of the Jury of the American Institute of Architects, Los Angeles, California.

1987   Member of the Jury of *Progressive Architecture* Magazine Awards.

2001   Member of the Master Jury of the Aga Khan Award for Architecture, Geneva, Switzerland.

VÍCTOR LEGORRETA

Born in Mexico City, on December 10, 1966.

EDUCATION

1990   B.A. in Architecture, Universidad Iberoamericana, Mexico City, Mexico.

PROFESSIONAL EXPERIENCE

1986   Works with Leason Pomeroy and Associates, Irvine, California.

1987   Works with Martorell, Bohigas and Mackay, Barcelona, Spain.

1988   Works with Fumihiko Maki, Tokyo, Japan.

1989   Enters Legorreta Arquitectos as project director.

1991   Partner in Legorreta Arquitectos (now Legorreta + Legorreta).

TEACHING EXPERIENCE

1995 - 2003   Lectures and seminars on Architecture in Mexico, the United States, Brazil, Colombia.

2002 -   Professor of project design, Universidad Iberoamericana, Mexico City, Mexico.

ARCHITECTURAL AWARDS JUROR

1998   Memberof the Jury of the American Institute of Architecture, Las Vegas, Nevada.

2000   Memberof the Jury of the American Institute of Architecture, Orange County, California.

2002   Member of the Jury of the AMDI (Mexican Association of Interior Design)

1	**2**	**3**	**4**
5	**6**	**7**	**8**
9	**10**	**11**	**12**	**13**
		14		
		15		**16**	**17**

1. Fumihiko Maki
2. Norman Foster
3. Richard Rogers
4. Charles Correa
5. From left to right:
   Lance Wyman, Mathias Goeritz,
   Alexander Calder, David Serur
6. Álvaro Siza
7. From left to right:
   Esteban San Juan, Rodolfo Morales,
   Francisco Toledo
8. Shigeru Ban
9. From left to right:
   Toshio Nakamura, Frank Gehry,
   Carter Brown, Ada Louise Huxtable,
   William Lacy, Giovanni Agnelli,
   Charles Correa
10. Eduardo Chillida
11. Moshe Safdie
12. From left to right:
    Sergio Hernández, Francisco Toledo
13. From left to right:
    Marek, Juan Soriano
14. Mario Pani
15. Richard Meier
16. From left to right:
    Fumihiko Maki, Cesar Pelli,
    Charles Correa
17. From left to right:
    Pedro Coronel, Alberto Gironella

Credit on Works

RICARDO LEGORRETA HOUSE / LOCATION: Mexico City, Mexico / AREA: 350 m^2 / DESIGN AND CONSTRUCTION PERIOD: 1996-1997 / ARCHITECTURE: Ricardo Legorreta / STURCTURAL DESIGN: Ricardo Camacho / ELECTRICAL DESIGN: Víctor Serrano / HYDRO-SANITARY DESIGN: Héctor Nieto / MECHANICAL DESIGN: CYVSA / LANDSCAPE DESIGN: Ricardo Legorreta / INTERIOR DESIGN: Ricardo Legorreta / **VISUAL ARTS CENTER, SANTA FE** / LOCATION: Santa fe, New Mexico / AREA: 9,800 m^2 / DESIGN AND CONSTRUCTION PERIOD: 1996-1999 / ASSOCIATED ARCHITECT: Lloyd & Tryk / STRUCTURAL DESIGN: Red Mountain Engineers / ELECTRICAL DESIGN: Bridgers & Paxton / HYDRO-SANITARY DESIGN: Bridgers & Paxton / INTERIOR DESIGN: LEGORRETA + LEGORRETA, Lloyd & Tryk / LANDSCAPE DESIGN: Design Workshop / CONTRACTOR: Bradbury & Stamm / **HOUSE IN ISRAEL** / LOCATION: Shfaim, Israel / AREA: 1,400 m^2 / DESIGN AND CONSTRUCTION PERIOD: 1995-2001 / ASSOCIATED ARCHITECT: Adolfo Levy / STRUCTURAL DESIGN: Buki Snir / ELECTRICAL DESIGN: Ytkin Blum / HYDRO-SANITARY DESIGN: Tavi Tesher / MECHANICAL DESIGN: Tavi Tesher / INTERIOR DESIGN: LEGORRETA + LEGORRETA, Armando Chávez, Jose Vigil / LANDSCAPE DESIGN: LEGORRETA + LEGORRETA / CONTRACTOR: Eli Shoshani / **HOUSE IN FLORIDA** / LOCATION: Hillsborough Beach, Florida / AREA : 2,300 m^2 / CONSTRUCTION PERIOD:1998-2002 / ASSOCIATED ARCHITECT: Bill Bernstein & Associates / LOCAL ARCHITECT: Sheriff & Associates / STRUCTURAL DESIGN: Derose and Slopey / ELECTRICAL DESIGN: Derose and Slopey / HYDRO-SANITARY DESIGN: Derose and Slopey / MECHANICAL DESIGN: Derose and Slopey / INTERIOR DESIGN: Gregga, Jordan, Smeszny / LANDSCAPE DESIGN: Fernando Caruncho / CONTRACTOR: Framme Steel & Company / **DORMITORIES, UNIVERSITY OF CHICAGO** / LOCATION: Chicago, Illinois / AREA: 22,500 m^2 / DESIGN AND CONSTRUCTION PERIOD: 1998-2001 / ASSOCIATED ARCHITECT: VOA Architects / STRUCTURAL DESIGN: Rubinos & Mesa Engineers / ELECTRICAL DESIGN: Primera Engineers Ltd. / HYDRO-SANITARY DESIGN: Primera Engineers Ltd. / MECHANICAL DESIGN: Primera Engineers Ltd. / INTERIOR DESIGN: LEGORRETA + LEGORRETA / LANDSCAPE DESIGN: Sasaki Associates, Inc. / CONTRACTOR: Pepper Construction / **DORMITORIES, STANFORD UNIVERSITY** / LOCATION: Palo Alto, California / AREA: 52,493 m^2 / DESIGN AND CONSTRUCTION PERIOD: 1995-1997 / ASSOCIATED ARCHITECT: The Steinberg Group / STRUCTURAL DESIGN: Dasee Design / ELECTRICAL DESIGN: OVE Arup & Partners / HYDRO-SANITARY DESIGN: OVE Arup & Partners / MECHANICAL DESIGN: OVE Arup & Partners / INTERIOR DESIGN: Brayton & Huges / LANDSCAPE DESIGN: Walker Johnson & Partners / CONTRACTOR: Linbeck / **LOS PATIOS I AND II RESIDENTIAL COMPOUND** / LOCATION: Lomas de Santa Fe, Mexico / AREA: 46,000 m^2 / DESIGN AND CONSTRUCTION PERIOD: Los Patios I, 1995-1998. Los Patios II, 1999-2002 / STRUCTURAL DESIGN: Decsa / ELECTRICAL DESIGN: Diin / HYDRO-SANITARY DESIGN: Diin / MECHANICAL DESIGN: Diin / LANDSCAPE DESIGN: Espacios Verdes, Eliseo Arredondo / CONTRACTOR: Constructora Tuca, S.A de C.V / **TELMEX TECHNOLOGY CENTER** / LOCATION: Mexico City, Mexico / ASSOCIATED ARCHITECT: Pablo Serrano / **TELEVISA SANTA FE** / LOCATION: Santa Fe, Mexico / AREA: 46,000 m^2 / DESIGN AND CONSTRUCTION PERIOD: 1990-1998 / STRUCTURAL DESIGN: Dirac / ELECTRICAL DESIGN: Hubbard & Burlon / HYDRO-SANITARY DESIGN: Inrasa / MECHANICAL DESIGN: Eclisa / INTERIOR DESIGN: LEGORRETA + LEGORRETA, Grupo Idea / LANDSCAPE DESIGN: Horacio Aguilar / CONTRACTOR: Gutsa / **LOMAS HOUSE** / LOCATION: Mexico City, Mexico / AREA: 712 m^2 / DESIGN AND CONSTRUCTION PERIOD: 1998-2000 / STRUCTURAL DESIGN: Decsa / ELECTRICAL DESIGN: Serdipar, S. A. de C. V. / HYDRO-SANITARY DESIGN: Serdipar, S. A. de C. V. / INTERIOR DESIGN: LEGORRETA + LEGORRETA / LANDSCAPE DESIGN: Espacios Verdes, S.A. de C.V / CONTRACTOR: Ayres, S. A. de C. V., ARCHITECTURE y Espacios / **HOUSE IN BRAZIL** / LOCATION: Barra do Una, Brazil / AREA: 28,000 m^2 / DESIGN AND CONSTRUCTION PERIOD: 1996-1998 / ASSOCIATED ARCHITECT: Gui Mattos / STRUCTURAL DESIGN: Benedictis Ingenieria / ELECTRICAL DESIGN: Gui Mattos Asociados / HYDRO-SANITARY DESIGN: Gui Mattos Asociados / INTERIOR DESIGN: LEGORRETA + LEGORRETA / LANDSCAPE DESIGN: LEGORRETA + LEGORRETA / CONTRACTOR: Marcelo Bruni / **HOUSE IN JAPAN** / LOCATION: Tokyo, Japan / AREA: 450 m^2 / DESIGN AND CONSTRUCTION PERIOD: 1996-1998 / ASSOCIATED ARCHITECT: Kajima Design (Atsu Wada, Yukishige Miyamae) / STRUCTURAL DESIGN: Kajima Design (Hiroaki Tomozumi) / ELECTRICAL DESIGN: Kajima Design, Keisuke Nakata / HYDRO-SANITARY DESIGN: Kajima Design, Hiroshi Hashimoto / MECHANICAL DESIGN: Kajima Design / INTERIOR DESIGN: LEGORRETA + LEGORRETA / LANDSCAPE DESIGN: LEGORRETA + LEGORRETA / CONTRACTOR: Kajima Corporation / MEXICAN PAVILION FOR **EXPO 2002** / LOCATION: Hannover, Germany / AREA: 2,714 m^2 / DESIGN AND CONSTRUCTION PERIOD: 1999-2000 / ASSOCIATED ARCHITECT: Tdm Architectos (Cristina Tellez, Marcela Valero) / LOCAL ARCHITECT: Bahlo, Kohnke, Stosberg & Partners / STRUCTURAL DESIGN: Eilers & Vogel Gmbh / ELECTRICAL DESIGN: Schmidt Reuter & Partners / HYDRO-SANITARY DESIGN: Schmidt Reuter & Partners / MECHANICAL DESIGN: Schmidt Reuter & Partners / CONTRACTOR: Arge / EXHIBITION DESIGN: Papalote Children's Museum (Marianela Servitje) / THEME COMPOSITION: Enrique Krauze / **ROOM FOR THE MILAN FURNITURE FAIR** / LOCATION: Milan, Italy / AREA: 32m^2 / DESIGN AND CONSTRUCTION PERIOD: 2001-2002 / ASSOCIATED ARCHITECT: Feg Industria Mobili / INTERIOR DESIGN: LEGORRETA + LEGORRETA / CONTRACTOR: Activa Design / **SHERATON ABANDOIBARRA** HOTEL / LOCATION: Bilbao, Spain / AREA: 16,400 m^2 / DESIGN AND CONSTRUCTION PERIOD: 1999- / ASSOCIATED ARCHITECT: Tdm Arquitectos (Cristina Téllez, Sandra Delgado) LOCAL ARCHITECT: Aurtenechea & Perez-Iriondo Arquitectos / STRUCTURAL DESIGN: Esteyco / ELECTRICAL DESIGN: Aguilera Ingenieros / HYDRO-SANITARY DESIGN: Aguilera Ingenieros / MECHANICAL DESIGN: Aguilera Ingenieros / INTERIOR DESIGN: LEGORRETA + LEGORRETA / CONTRACTOR: Fonorte / **HOUSE OF THE 15 PATIOS** / LOCATION: Mexico City, Mexico / AREA: 1,257 m^2 / DESIGN AND CONSTRUCTION PERIOD: 1996-1998 / ASSOCIATED ARCHITECT: Armando Chávez, Jose Vigil / STRUCTURAL DESIGN: Ricardo Camacho / ELECTRICAL DESIGN: Alejandro Borgoa / HYDRO-SANITARY DESIGN: Carlos Turco / MECHANICAL DESIGN: Alejandro Borgoa / INTERIOR DESIGN: LEGORRETA + LEGORRETA / LANDSCAPE DESIGN: Eliseo Arredondo / CONTRACTOR: Miguel Campero / **RENO HOUSE** / LOCATION: Reno, Nevada / AREA: 1,658 m^2 / DESIGN AND CONSTRUCTION PERIOD: 1997-1999 / ASSOCIATED ARCHITECT: Stay Architecture & Design (Walter Stay) / STRUCTURAL DESIGN: Ferrari Associates / ELECTRICAL DESIGN: Pinchale Engineering / MECHANICAL DESIGN: Peterson & Associates / INTERIOR DESIGN: LEGORRETA + LEGORRETA / LANDSCAPE DESIGN: LEGORRETA + LEGORRETA / CONTRACTOR: Frank Bleuss / **TECHNOLOGICAL MUSEUM OF INNOVATION** / LOCATION: San Jose, California/ AREA: 11,000 m^2 / DESIGN AND CONSTRUCTION PERIOD: 1996- / ASSOCIATED ARCHITECT: The Steinberg Group / STRUCTURAL DESIGN: Rinne + Peterson / ELECTRICAL DESIGN: Fisher Marantz Renfro Stone—Arrigoni & Associates Inc. / HYDRO-SANITARY DESIGN: Guttman + Mac Ritchie / MECHANICAL DESIGN: Guttman + Mac Ritchie / INTERIOR DESIGN: SMWM, LEGORRETA + LEGORRETA / **HOUSES IN EL TAMARINDO: LA CRUZ HOUSE** / LOCATION: Puerto Vallarta, Mexico / AREA: 1,475 m^2 / DESIGN AND CONSTRUCTION PERIOD: 1997- 2000 / STRUCTURAL DESIGN: Decsa / ELECTRICAL DESIGN: SERDIPAR, S.A de C.V / HYDRO-SANITARY DESIGN: Ingenieria y Proyectos Hidromecánicos S.A. / MECHANICAL DESIGN: Dypro / INTERIOR DESIGN: LEGORRETA + LEGORRETA / LANDSCAPE DESIGN: LEGORRETA + LEGORRETA / CONTRACTOR: Grupo Plan / **LAS TERRAZAS HOUSE** / LOCATION: Puerto Vallarta, Mexico / AREA: 1,160 m^2 / DESIGN AND CONSTRUCTION PERIOD: 1999- 2001 / STRUCTURAL DESIGN: Decsa, Ricardo Camacho / ELECTRICAL DESIGN: Serdipar, S. A. de C. V. / HYDRO-SANITARY DESIGN: Ingenieria y proyectos Hidromecánicos S. A. / MECHANICAL DESIGN: Dypro / INTERIOR DESIGN: LEGORRETA + LEGORRETA / LANDSCAPE DESIGN: LEGORRETA + LEGORRETA / CONTRACTOR: Grupo Plan / **EGADE** / LOCATION: Monterrey, Mexico / AREA: 8,000 m^2 / DESIGN AND CONSTRUCTION PERIOD: 1999-2001 / ASSOCIATED ARCHITECT: Juan Carlos Pérez / STRUCTURAL DESIGN: ITESM, Engineering Department / ELECTRICAL DESIGN: Tecnos Ing. S. A. / HYDRO-SANITARY DESIGN: Tecnos, Ing. S. A. / MECHANICAL DESIGN: Termocontrol del norte, Barrenechea / INTERIOR DESIGN: LEGORRETA + LEGORRETA / LANDSCAPE DESIGN: LEGORRETA + LEGORRETA / CONTRACTOR: Tec. de Monterrey / **AMERICAN UNIVERSITY IN CAIRO** / LOCATION: Cairo, Egypt / AREA: 16,000 m^2 / DESIGN AND CONSTRUCTION PERIOD: 2001- / ASSOCIATED ARCHITECT: Saleh Hamdy / STRUCTURAL DESIGN: Eco Engineering Consultancy Office / ELECTRICAL DESIGN: Shaker Consultancy Group / HYDRO-SANITARY DESIGN: Shaker Consultancy Group / MECHANICAL DESIGN: Shaker Consultancy Group / INTERIOR DESIGN: Luchetti Associates/Sites International / LANDSCAPE DESIGN: Carol R. Jonson Associates/Sites International / CONTRACTOR: Flour Daniels / ENVIRONMENTAL CONSULTANT: HL–Technik AG / **APARTMENT IN MEXICO CITY** / LOCATION: Mexico City, Mexico / AREA: 600 m^2 / DESIGN AND CONSTRUCTION PERIOD: 2001-2002 / ELECTRICAL DESIGN: Serdipar / HYDRO-SANITARY DESIGN: Serdipar / MECHANICAL DESIGN: Cyvsa / INTERIOR DESIGN: LEGORRETA + LEGORRETA / CONTRACTOR: Miguel Gómez / **HOUSE IN HAWAII** / LOCATION: Maui, Hawaii / AREA: 2,500 m^2 / DESIGN AND CONSTRUCTION PERIOD: 2000-2002 / ARCHITECTURE: LEGORRETA + LEGORRETA / ASSOCIATED ARCHITECT: Marcela Cortina / LOCAL ARCHITECT: Sha Kawasaki Architects (Harish Shah, Geddes Ulinskas) / STRUCTURAL DESIGN: Walter Vorfeld Associates (Walter Vorfeld) / ELECTRICAL DESIGN: C & B Consulting Engineers / HYDRO-SANITARY DESIGN: C&B Consulting Engineers / MECHANICAL DESIGN: LRB C&B Consulting Engineers (Paul O´Neil, Enrico Martín) / INTERIOR DESIGN: The Wiseman Group / LANDSCAPE DESIGN: Suzman Design Associates / CONTRACTOR: Ryan Associates (Paul Ryan, John Royson, Mark Klinzman) / **CHIRON LIFE AND SCIENCE LABORATORIES** / LOCATION: Emeryville City, California / AREA: 26,000 m^2 / DESIGN AND CONSTRUCTION PERIOD: 1998 / ASSOCIATED ARCHITECT: Flad & Associates / STRUCTURAL DESIGN: Flad & Associates / ELECTRICAL DESIGN: AEI Engineers / HYDRO-SANITARY DESIGN: AEI Engineers / MECHANICAL DESIGN: AEI Engineers / INTERIOR DESIGN: LEGORRETA + LEGORRETA, Brayton & Huges / LANDSCAPE DESIGN: Peter Walker William Johnson & Partners / CONTRACTOR: Rudolph & Sletten / **EL ROBLE OFFICE BUILDING** / LOCATION: Escazú, Costa Rica / AREA: 48,240 m^2 / DESIGN AND CONSTRUCTION PERIOD: Begun in 1999 / ASSOCIATED ARCHITECT: Grupo Roble (Avi Aviram) / STRUCTURAL DESIGN: Tecnoconsult (Juan Carlos Ulate) / ELECTRICAL DESIGN: Tecnoconsult / HYDRO-SANITARY DESIGN: Tecnoconsult / MECHANICAL DESIGN: Tecnoconsult / LANDSCAPE DESIGN: Proverde / CONTRACTOR: Van Der Laat and Jiménez / **PARQUE EUROPA** / LOCATION: Madrid, Spain / AREA: 7,000 m^2 / ASSOCIATED ARCHITECTS: Benjamín González and Jorge Covarrubias / LOCAL ARCHITECT: Aguinaga y Asociados / **CABERNET HOUSE** / LOCATION: Santa Helena, California / AREA: 15,548 m^2 / DESIGN AND CONSTRUCTION PERIOD: 1996-1999 / ASSOCIATED ARCHITECT: Walker/Warner Architects (Brooks, Walker, Kevin Killen) / STRUCTURAL DESIGN: MKM Associates / MECHANICAL DESIGN: Sterk Engineering / INTERIOR DESIGN: LEGORRETA + LEGORRETA / CONTRACTOR: Cello & Madru Construction (Bill Madru) / **HACIENDA IN SÃO PAULO** / LOCATION: São Paulo, Brazil / AREA: 2,500 m^2 / DESIGN AND CONSTRUCTION PERIOD: 2001- / ASSOCIATED ARCHITECT: Ricardo Lemus Furtado / STRUCTURAL DESIGN: Aluzio a.m. D´avila / ELECTRICAL DESIGN: MHA Engenharia Ltda / HYDRO-SANITARY DESIGN: MHA Engenharia Ltda. / MECHANICAL DESIGN: MHA Engenharia Ltda. / INTERIOR DESIGN: LEGORRETA + LEGORRETA , Claudia Moreira Salles / LANDSCAPE DESIGN: Fernando Chacel / CONTRACTOR: Método, Martín Miguel Daniel / **HOUSE NEAR A LAKE** / LOCATION: Valle de Bravo, Mexico / AREA: 1,200 m^2 / DESIGN AND CONSTRUCTION PERIOD: 2000-2002 / ASSOCIATED ARCHITECT: Alejandro Danel / STRUCTURAL DESIGN: Ricardo Camacho / ELECTRICAL DESIGN: Víctor Serrano / HYDRO-SANITARY DESIGN: Víctor Serrano / INTERIOR DESIGN: LEGORRETA + LEGORRETA / LANDSCAPE DESIGN: Eliseo Arredondo / CONTRACTOR: Genaro Nieto / **JUÁREZ SQUARE** / LOCATION: Mexico City, Mexico / AREA: 100,000 m^2 / DESIGN AND CONSTRUCTION PERIOD: 2002- / STRUCTURAL DESIGN: Raul Izquierdo / ELECTRICAL DESIGN: Piesa / HYDRO-SANITARY DESIGN: Garza Maldonado y Asociados / CONTRACTOR: Grupo Farla / FOUNTAIN DESIGN: Vicente Rojo / **VÍCTOR LEGORRETA HOUSE** / LOCATION: Valle de Bravo, Mexico / AREA: 450 m^2 / DESIGN AND CONSTRUCTION PERIOD: 2001-2002 / ARCHITECTURE: Víctor Legorreta / ASSOCIATED ARCHITECT: Alejandro Danel / STRUCTURAL DESIGN: Decsa (Ricardo Camacho) / ELECTRICAL DESIGN: Serdipar (Víctor Serrano) / HYDRO-SANITARY DESIGN: Serdipar (Víctor Serrano) / MECHANICAL DESIGN: Serdipar (Víctor Serrano) / INTERIOR DESIGN: Víctor Legorreta / LANDSCAPE DESIGN: Eliseo Arredondo / CONTRACTOR: Efrén Emeterio / **ZANDRA RHODES MUSEUM** / LOCATION: London, England / AREA: 2,546 m^2 / DESIGN AND CONSTRUCTION PERIOD: 2000-2001 / ASSOCIATED ARCHITECT: Alan Camp Architects (Alan Camp, Martin Crowley, Andy Kinder, Achim Linde) / STRUCTURAL DESIGN: Packman Lucas / ELECTRICAL DESIGN: Helix Services Consultancy / HYDRO-SANITARY DESIGN: Helix Services Consultancy / MECHANICAL DESIGN: Helix Services Consultancy / CONTRACTOR: Glimac / **ITESM SANTA FE** / LOCATION: Mexico City, Mexico / AREA: 34,000 m^2 / DESIGN AND CONSTRUCTION PERIOD: 2000-2001 / ASSOCIATED ARCHITECT: Arquitectos Asociados S.C., Imanol Ordorica / STRUCTURAL DESIGN: Correa Hermanos / ELECTRICAL DESIGN: Piesa, S. A. de C. V. / HYDRO-SANITARY DESIGN: IRYMSA, S. A. de C. V. / MECHANICAL DESIGN: Tec. de Monterrey / INTERIOR DESIGN: LEGORRETA + LEGORRETA / LANDSCAPE DESIGN: LEGORRETA + LEGORRETA / CONTRACTOR: Tec de Monterrey.

Photography Credits

HOUSE IN JAPAN, TOKYO, 1998.

LEGORRETA + LEGORRETA

Printed in 2003 in Japan
by Toppan Printing Co., Ltd.

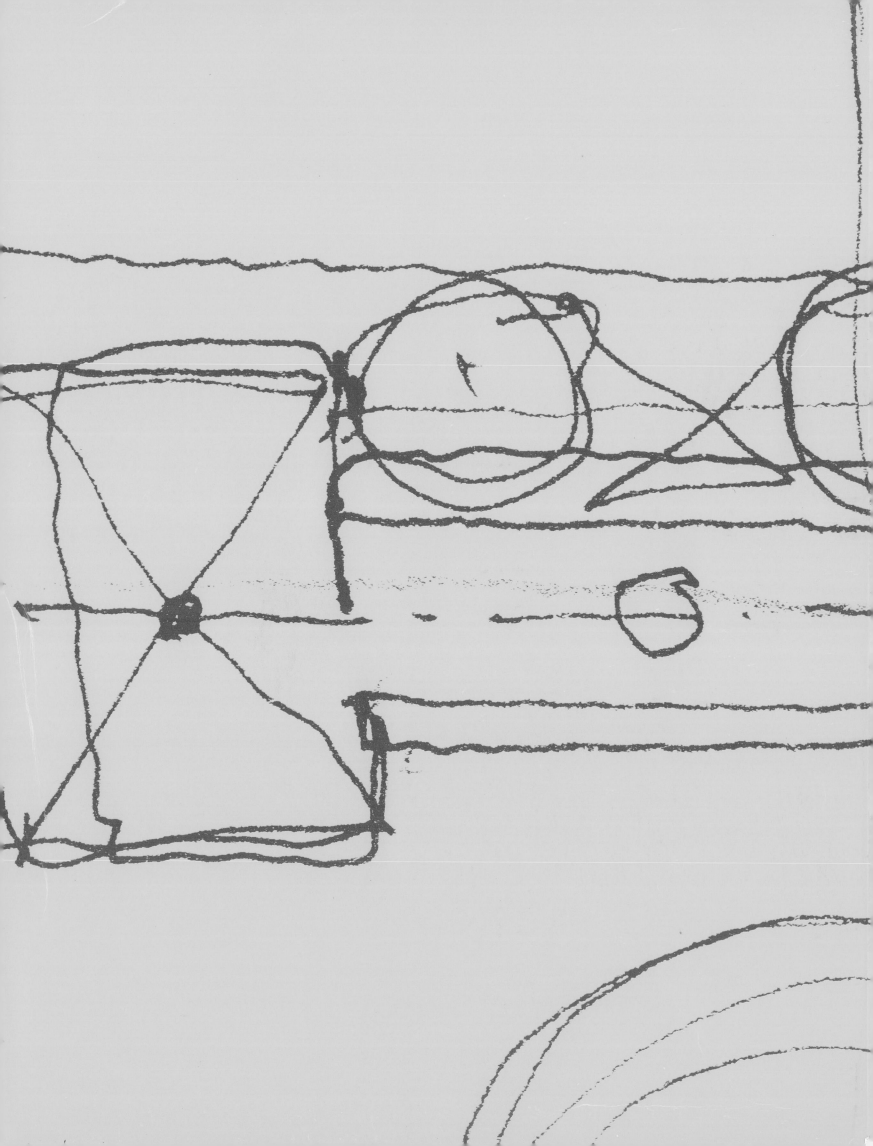